Mission
FORSAKEN

John D. Murphy

The University of Phoenix
Affair With Wall Street

Mission
FORSAKEN

PROVING GROUND EDUCATION

Published by Proving Ground Education

ISBN: 978-0-9669683-1-6 (paperback)
ISBN: 978-0-9669683-2-3 (ebook / ePub)
ISBN: 978-0-9669683-3-0 (ebook / Kindle & Mobi)

Get the right digital edition for your favorite eReader: Get the ePub for iPads and B&N Nook, and Mobi for Kindle and the Sony eReader.

Cover design by Illusion Factory

Page design by DesignForBooks.com

Thanks to Sue and John Morris at Editide, Vermont, and to Julia Wilk for additional research. Special thanks to Paula Key.

There must be considered that there is nothing more difficult to carry out, nor more doubtful of success, nor more dangerous than to initiate a new order of things. For the innovator has enemies in all of those who would profit by the old order and only lukewarm defenders in all those who would profit by the new order. This lukewarmness arising partly from fear of their opponents who have the laws in their favor and partly from the skepticism of mankind who do not truly believe in anything new until they have had actual experience at it.

—NICOLO MACHIAVELLI[1]

Life is, in fact, a battle. Evil is innocent and strong; beauty enchanting but rare; folly very apt to be defiant; wickedness to carry the day; imbeciles to be in great places; people of sense in small, and mankind generally unhappy. But the world as it stands is no narrow illusion, no phantasm, no evil dream of the night; we wake up to it again forever and ever; and we can neither forget it or deny it, nor dispense with it.

—HENRY JAMES[2]

Academe, n. An ancient school where morality and philosophy were taught.
Academy, n. A modern school where football is taught.

—AMBROSE BIERCE[3]

Contents

Introduction ix

Part One: Founding and Rite of Passage

Foreword 3

1. Improbable Collaboration 5
2. Crucible of Survival 19
3. Phoenix Ascendant 33
4. The Creation of The University of Phoenix 41
5. Candidacy for Accreditation—Educational Model for Working Adults 53
6. Teaching/Learning Model 69
7. Perception Issues 79
8. Accreditation—Arizona Regents' Attack 91
9. "Education Is Not as Sudden as a Massacre" 103
10. Evaluation for Accreditation 115
11. Arizona Regents' Attempts to Secede from North Central—AACRAO 123

12. Forces Within/Forces Without 131

13. "Egregious" College 141

14. California Political Theater 151

15. Golden State Legislative Fight 163

16. Establishment Taps Out 169

17. Other Regulatory and Legislative Conflicts 177

18. Home Front 183

Part Two: Mission Forsaken

Foreword 193

19. Beginning of the End and the End 195

20. Educational Mission 207

Part Three: Gainful Education

Gainful Education 217

Appendices

I: The Butterball Effect 245

II: North Central Commission on Institutions of Higher Education Paper on Regional Accreditation Issues 251

III: 2000-2013 Regulatory, Legislative, and Legal Actions With the University of Phoenix and Apollo Group 257

Endnotes 259

Introduction

The Institution that Changed American Higher Education Forever

In 1976, what became the University of Phoenix applied for candidacy for accreditation from the Commission on Institutions of Higher Education—now Higher Learning Commission—of the North Central Association of Colleges and Schools. One of the two oldest, the largest, and the most prestigious of the regional accrediting associations in the United States, North Central accredits public and private primary, secondary, and postsecondary institutions in nineteen states, including Arizona.

Three distinguished traditional academics made up the team that evaluated the University of Phoenix for candidacy. Team chair, Dr. Donald Roush, was Academic Vice President of New Mexico State University, Las Cruces, and the former president of the North Central Association. Dr. Wade Ellis was Associate Dean of the Graduate School at the University of Michigan, and Dr. Roy Trout, President of the University for Sciences and the Arts of Oklahoma.

This marked the first time the North Central Association evaluated a for-profit, nontraditional academic degree-granting institution that integrated higher education with the lives of the students, rather than the students integrating their lives with higher education. In the summer of 1977, based on the scrutiny of a University of Phoenix institutional self-study and on-site evaluation, the visiting team recommended candidacy.

The University of Phoenix visiting team report was evaluated, like every other report upon which such recommendations are based, by a North Central Review Committee made up of individuals outside the state of the institution being evaluated. The review committee affirmed the recommendation of the evaluation team, and the North Central commission—after an examination of the evaluation corpus—granted the University of Phoenix candidacy.

Reaction of Arizona State University System

In the troubled minds of key leaders and their minions in the Arizona state university system, the granting of candidacy to an allegedly unknown, newly Arizona-based, nontraditional for-profit institution with no campus, no library, and a faculty who worked full time in other professions was incontrovertible evidence that North Central had abandoned its accreditation standards. This leaden belief resulted in pitched efforts by the Arizona state university system to upend the accreditation of the University of Phoenix by publicly characterizing it as a diploma mill and attempting to compromise the integrity of the accreditation process by leveraging its political status as a public university system with the North Central Commission on Institutions of Higher Education.

Due, in some part, to the Arizona state university system's heavy-handed political interference with North Central, the University of Phoenix was awarded accreditation during its second year of candidacy. The behavior of the Arizona state university system helped ensure the accreditation of the University of Phoenix in two rather than the customary five years.

University of Phoenix and Apollo Group

Three years after the University of Phoenix was accredited, it established a holding company, Apollo Group, Inc., that permitted changes in ownership and control without triggering North Central and U.S. Department of Education reaccreditation requirements, and could be brought public independent of North Central approval.

After eighteen years of incremental but sustained academic and financial success at the University of Phoenix, Apollo Group went public. Apollo's stunning financial success ultimately caused the wheels to come off high graduation rates, low student loan default rates, effective regulatory management, and the attraction of substantial tuition revenue from the private sector.

Replacement of Revenue Source

When Apollo Group went public, 80 percent of University of Phoenix's working adult students—average age mid-thirties with an average of nine years or more of employment—received employer tuition reimbursement: 84 percent had at least one-half of their tuition reimbursed and 42 percent received full reimbursement.[4]

By 2009, almost 87 percent of Apollo Group's revenue—90 percent from the University of Phoenix—was from federal taxpayer sources.[5] University of Phoenix Pell Grant revenue in 2001 was $24 million; by 2011, it had grown to $1.2 billion.[6]

Because of becoming publicly traded and later forsaking its founding mission, revenue from the private sector was almost totally supplanted by revenue from American taxpayers.

Elimination of Founding Admissions Standards

The seemingly limitless growth in federal student loan and Pell Grant revenue constituted a sea change in University of Phoenix student demographics. It resulted from the elimination of admissions standards that defined and facilitated the achievement of its founding educational mission of solely serving working adult learners. These standards helped ensure that all admitted were capable of benefiting gainfully from a teaching/learning model with an applied rather than theoretical learning focus.

This was not the only consequence of the Apollo/University of Phoenix/Wall Street smoking hot spreadsheet bliss.

Prior to and at the time of the Apollo Group IPO, the University of Phoenix undergraduate graduation rate stood near 65 percent, equaling and even exceeding traditional nonprofit and public colleges and universities. The average national postsecondary student loan default rate was then 15 percent, and at the University of Phoenix, about 5 percent.[7]

The University of Phoenix Consumer Guide 2011—2012, indicates its graduation rate for bachelor's programs in cohort year 2005, was 33 percent after six years.[8] The U.S. Department of Education Integrated Postsecondary Education Data System (IPEDS) reports University of

Phoenix graduation rates for bachelor's programs as follows: 2004—9 percent; 2005—7 percent; 2006—14 percent; 2007—11 percent; 2008—13 percent; 2009—14 percent; 2010—13 percent; and 2011—13 percent.[9]

The student loan default rate for the cohort year ending September 30 was: 2007—15.9 percent; 2008—21.1 percent; and 2009—26.4 percent.[10] University of Phoenix withdrawal rate for students using post-9/11 GI Bill funds were 50 percent in bachelor's programs, and 66 percent in associate's programs.[11]

Being a Wall Street squeeze manifested in one other deeply disquieting way.

From its founding until 1999, the University of Phoenix never received a federal or state regulatory fine, or was the target or the victim of whistleblower lawsuits or legal judgments. Between 1999 and 2013, Apollo Group and its subsidiaries paid some $242 million in fines and judgments.[12]

Ten-Year Accreditation-to-Accreditation Probation

In 2002, the University of Phoenix received a reaffirmation of accreditation visit by the North Central Higher Learning Commission. It resulted, for the first time in its history, in a ten-year accreditation. The reaffirmation of accreditation evaluation visit ten years later resulted in a recommendation for accreditation probation.

In 2004,[13] the University of Phoenix forsook—in favor of an open admissions policy—its mission of solely serving working adult students by eliminating its founding admissions criteria tied to age, full-time employment, and experience. The same as at a tax-supported community college, virtually any eighteen-year-old with a high school diploma or GED now qualified for enrollment. Axia

College, a primarily online, associate degree-granting institution established in the Apollo Group subsidiary, Western International University, in 2004, was made part of the University of Phoenix in 2006, and the associate degree subgroup became targeted for enrollment.

The demographic shift in the composition of its student body and revenue source profile arose from the admission of individuals employed—if employed at all—at entities without employee educational benefits. Admission to an accredited institution typically results in automatic qualification for federally guaranteed student loans and grants, and a significant percentage of students admitted under the open admissions policy relied on taxpayer funds to underwrite the cost of attendance.

Despite the magnitude of the change in admissions standards absolutely destined to result in the major alteration in student demographics and thus mission, the University of Phoenix North Central Statement of Affiliation Status—which publicly documents all material accrediting actions—does not reflect the application of North Central Substantive Change criteria prior to this sea change in mission being implemented.

The admissions standards that defined and facilitated the achievement of the University of Phoenix educational mission since its founding almost thirty-five years earlier were eliminated.

The North Central Association of Colleges and Schools Higher Learning Commission declined to identify the action it took when the University of Phoenix materially changed its founding mission, or when it added Axia, other than noting that its Substantive Change criteria has been revised.[14]

Accreditation Probation

Following the ten-year North Central evaluation visit in 2012, the visiting team recommended—because it determined that the University of Phoenix failed to meet one or more criteria for accreditation—that it be placed on accreditation probation. The North Central Higher Learning Commission will affirm the visiting team's recommendation or issue a different finding of fact, and issue a final ruling in 2013.

Apollo Group

Apollo Group remains the largest enterprise in the American for-profit postsecondary sector. In 2009, Apollo allocated its revenue—almost 87 percent from federal taxpayer sources—as follows:

- $1,005,935,000 ($2,535 per student) on profit
- $ 935,476,000 ($2,225 per student) on marketing, and
- $ 374,899,997 ($892 per student) on instruction.[15]

When Apollo Group stock reached a five-year high of $90 per share in 2009, an Apollo executive allowed

> *[A] feeling was building in everyone's stomach: . . . it felt too good.*

The result was to overhaul

> *. . . its grow-at-any-costs admissions practices.*[16]

The integration of Axia College into the University of Phoenix coupled with the open admissions policy more than doubled student head count for a period of time. It was a money-spinning financial decision, but a cheerless academic disaster: Axia

> *failed to graduate many of the thousands of unprepared students it had relentlessly enrolled in mostly online programs, leaving them with student loan debts they couldn't pay.*[17]

The failure stirred an Apollo executive to acknowledge the problem publicly: *I think we lost our way a bit.*[18]

Profits and market capitalization at Apollo had skyrocketed. Financial benefits were highly lucrative to Apollo voting shareholders and executives. Between 2004 and 2012, Apollo voting shareholders John Sperling and his son sold approximately $727 million in Apollo stock, while its directors and executives liqudated approximately $85 million.[19]

High academic persistence, low student-loan default rates, and the absence of regulatory and legal sanctions and judgments were no longer the fountain of prideful accomplishment.

For-Profit Status and Survival

Counterintuitively, one of the primary reasons the University of Phoenix survived implacable opposition by some in traditional higher education is precisely because it is for profit.

The University of Phoenix once proudly asserted that because of its for-profit status, it should and could be held accountable for educational quality and the academic achievements of its students, something that is almost impossible to exact at taxpayer-funded, traditional public higher education institutions. This accountability helped ensure its survival when it could have—and nearly did more than once during its first fifteen years—ceased existence on any given day.

The University of Phoenix would be long gone if only one of four working adult students whose employers once underwrote all or part of their tuition ever graduated.

Change in Admissions Procedures

In response to continued criticism of the for-profit sector because of low graduation and high student-loan default rates, in 2011, the U.S. Department of Education imposed new restrictions on student-recruiter compensation. The University of Phoenix responded by requiring undergraduate applicants to complete a mandatory three-week orientation as a condition of being admitted. This orientation caused a precipitous decline in student census: some 450,000 students in 2011 fell to some 300,000 students by 2013.

The change in admissions procedures appears to validate the criticism that, following the adoption of the open admissions policy and incorporating Axia College into its academic world, the University of Phoenix admitted tens of thousands of individuals incapable of gainful education. They were incapable because they were attending an institution designed solely for working adults with a teaching/learning model with an applied, rather than theoretical curriculum, an active rather than passive classroom learning environment, and taught by seasoned practitioners with advanced academic degrees.

They were wildebeests in a river of crocodiles.

The steep decline in student census also caused a precipitous drop in the value of Apollo stock from which it is yet to recover. The University of Phoenix closed more than half of its physical locations in late 2012, and now in 2013, its accreditation is in question.

Hard-Fought Political History of the University of Phoenix

The history of the University of Phoenix is an odyssey of educational entrepreneurship in a sector of society with a congenital resistance to innovation and change; a cautionary tale of what can happen when the financial values of the corporate world are applied to the provision of postsecondary education with an outmoded regulatory system; and what can occur when proven educational principles elemental to the achievement of a singular educational mission appear to have been sacrificed on the altar of commerce with the pro forma approval of a regional accrediting association.

From its founding, and continuing for more than two decades, the University of Phoenix triumphed repeatedly over nearly insuperable opposition from traditional higher education: state boards of regents, postsecondary education commissions, traditional private and public higher education institutions, public higher education systems, state legislatures, regional and programmatic accrediting associations, traditional higher education membership organizations, a few reactionary academics, and an often unfriendly and superficially critical media.

The signature outcome of this truly remarkable and sometimes hair-raising odyssey of survival through the diligence of hard political will, was that the University of Phoenix became recognized nationally as the "gold standard" in nontraditional academic degree education for working adults.

Nearly twenty years of vetting academic quality and the achievement of its mission by its accrediting association, programmatic accrediting associations, and state licensing agencies proved to be the foundation for the highly successful public offering by its holding company, Apollo Group. The offering unleashed the ungodly growth in Apollo stock by thousands and thousands of percent during the decade even prior to the forsaking of the mission that was the foundation of its well-earned and respected academic and financial successes.

Despite hard-fought victories anchored to steadfast fidelity to the University of Phoenix teaching/learning model for working adults, growth in the value of Apollo stock appears to have become the *sine qua non* of its existence. It transubstantiated in part through the selection of sales, marketing, and investment-banking professionals for its most highly compensated executive management positions. The values, beliefs, and skills that typically accompany such often-talented individuals provided the philosophical and practical basis for forsaking its historical admissions standards, and thus the founding mission of the University of Phoenix.

The far-reaching and potentially—now painfully manifested—negative consequences were not taken into appropriate consideration because of the apparent failure of the North Central Association to properly and objectively interpret and apply its Substantive Change criteria prior to these sea changes being implemented at the University of Phoenix. According to the University of Phoenix's calculations, nearly 70 percent of those in bachelor's programs since 2003 failed to graduate after eight years.[20]

"Gold Standard" Status

Arguably, the *quid pro quo* for Apollo's truly dazzling financial success accompanying the forsaking of the University of Phoenix's founding mission is the sacrifice of its hard-earned "gold standard" reputation and standing as the premier degree-granting institution for working adults that once attracted enthusiastic, loyal, and generous private sector corporate financial support through the payment of employee tuition.

A shameful and decidedly unfair price was and is being paid by hundreds of thousands of University of Phoenix working adult graduates who have been subjected to the scandal-ridden decline in the well-earned reputation and standing of their alma mater due to disgraceful declines in the percentage of students completing degrees, embarrassing percentages of student-loan defaults, reprehensible payment of millions of dollars in regulatory fines and whistleblower judgments, the shuttering of half of its campuses, and the now abhorrent possibility of its accreditation placed on notice.

Dedication

This personal account and interpretation of this odyssey of nontraditional higher education survival, success, and excess is dedicated to every working adult student who earned a University of Phoenix degree.

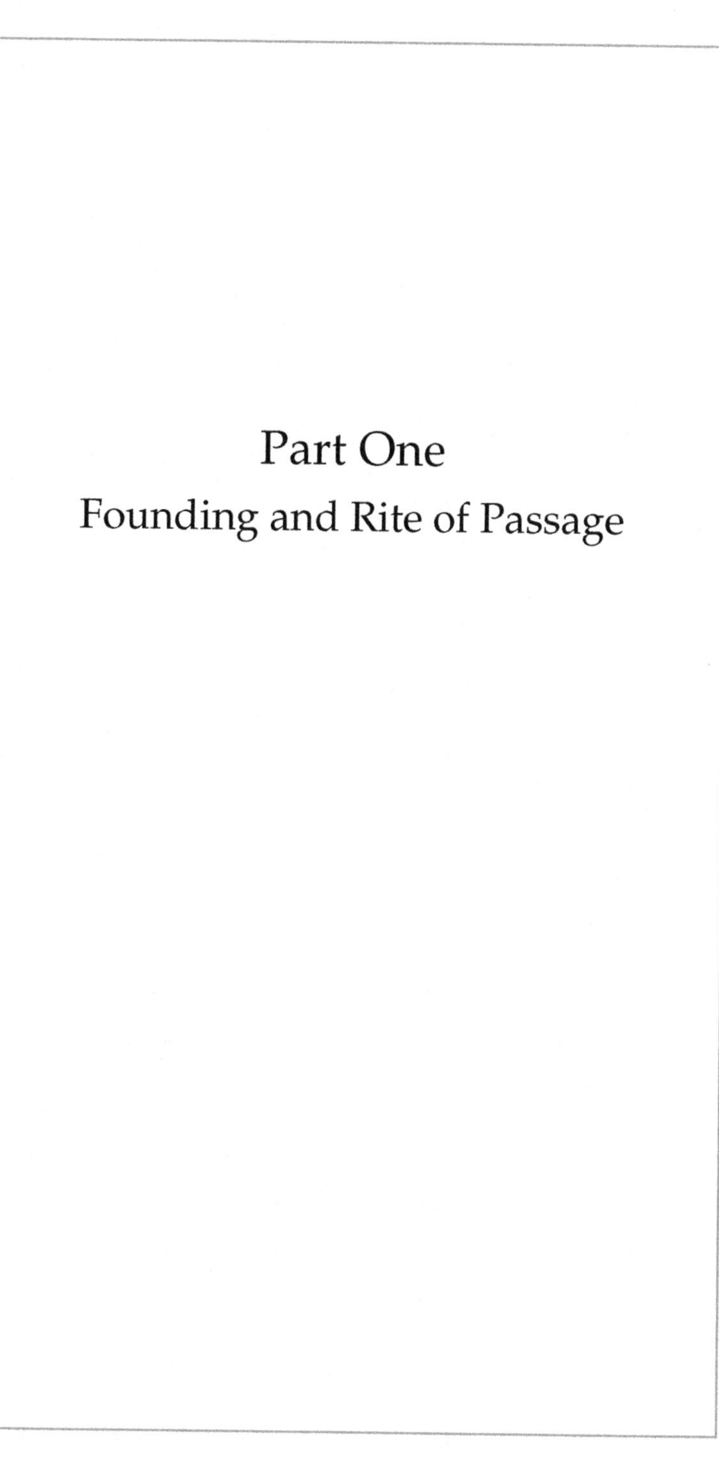

Part One

Founding and Rite of Passage

Foreword

The University of Phoenix enrolled eight working adult students when accredited by the Commission on Institutions of Higher Education—subsequently renamed the Higher Learning Commission—of the North Central Association of Colleges and Schools. It now enrolls over 300,000 students and has 700,000 graduates.

In numerical company with the New York and California state university systems, the University of Phoenix is one of the largest private accredited higher education institutions in the world.

The University of Phoenix went public through its holding company, Apollo Group, and spawned a publicly traded, multibillion-dollar for-profit sector of the educational-industrial complex. This sector now dominates growth in postsecondary education enrollment, percentage of federally guaranteed student loans for its number of students, and student-loan default rates.

The University of Phoenix was granted candidacy for accreditation and became—*sui generis*—the bête noir of many well placed in traditional higher education. It faced moral opposition because it is a private for-profit enterprise in an industry monopolized by nonprofit and public institutions. It faced philosophical opposition because its founding teaching/learning model and educational delivery system for full-time working adults violated virtually every standard of traditional American higher education.

Innovation is largely philosophical confetti in traditional higher education when unaccompanied by the enthusiasm for dirtying one's hands by protecting it politically. Successful innovation is rooted in the commitment of its innovators to fight for it, regardless of the form of opposition or obstacles in its path. The University of Phoenix prevailed against stunningly impossible odds because its founders never turned away from any challenge and once maintained absolute fidelity to its founding principles.

Every success or failure story is an intensely human one and this odyssey of higher education innovation is no different. What is different is the overwhelming and sometimes startling nature of the survival of a nontraditional higher education institution, its extraordinary educational and financial successes, and what resulted from the forsaking of its hard-fought founding mission.

CHAPTER

1

Improbable Collaboration

This University of Phoenix odyssey turns in some measure on the improbable collaboration between two men in the founding, development, and political protection of an innovative, nontraditional for-profit higher education institution for working adults.

I grew up in an upper-middle-class neighborhood on the San Francisco, California, peninsula, and spent much of my youth on the tennis courts and in the swimming pool of a country club in a zip code with one of the highest per capita incomes in the United States.

John G. Sperling barely survived the Great Depression in a log cabin in a hard cob Missouri Ozark hamlet. His childhood was spent agonizing whether there would be anything to eat and being beaten serially by an alcoholic father who failed at most everything except creating children.

My father was a sober, talented, playful, personable, and highly successful marketing and sales executive, born in the Midwest, proud of providing for a stay-at-home mother and three sons. One great grandfather was a principal in the Comstock mine in Virginia City, Nevada, and counted Mark Twain among his friends.

We shared blue-collar experiences. Sperling worked on ocean-going freighters in the merchant marine, and while in college, I on a Long Beach, California, wharf as a summer member of the Teamsters' union. At high school graduation we were semiliterate. Sperling earned a doctorate at the University of Cambridge in England, and I degrees from the California state higher education system and a private university.

We met at a third-tier state university in California in the early 1970s where Sperling was a tenured professor of humanities and I—when an undergraduate—founded a community mental health project with ex-state mental hospital patients abandoned in the campus community when Governor Reagan closed California's state mental hospitals.

Besides differences in age and educational pedigree, when together, we looked funny. I'm six two and a half and 220 pounds, Sperling five seven and 150 pounds. He brightened the physical anomaly by often sporting a Greek fisherman's cap.

I joined John to earn accreditation from one of the most highly regarded regional accrediting associations in the United States. Seeking accreditation commenced a collaboration, mentorship, and friendship that thrived nearly two decades.

Five years before I resigned my senior executive position and voting ownership from the private university that had been brought public through its holding company, I committed an act of the heart that ended my relationship with John Sperling, the private university, and the holding company into which I then had invested most of my adult life.

Arizona

I moved from San Jose, California, to Phoenix, Arizona, in late 1977 to help John Sperling found the University of Phoenix. I can be seduced by impossible odds and was openly optimistic about the ground-floor development of a nontraditional higher education institution solely for working adults. I remained confident that by creativity, relentless hard work, and intellectual collaboration with John Sperling and some fellow state university alums, we could overcome virtually any challenge.

Five months prior to my move to Phoenix, the North Central Association of Colleges and Schools accepted the University of Phoenix as a candidate for accreditation.

On Sunday, the day after my arrival, brimming with hope and aglow with promise, I joined John and a girlfriend and collaborator, Carole Crawford, for breakfast at her condominium across from an Arizona National Guard base. I picked up the *Arizona Republic* on the way. The thick Sunday paper sat on the counter while we ate; none of us had even glanced at it.

Why would the flagship Arizona newspaper contain anything about a nontraditional university with eight working adult students that had been granted accreditation candidacy from the same entity that accredited all educational institutions in the state?

I don't remember who caught the headline, but we were all floored: *'Quick-degrees' college in line for accreditation.*[21]

In a lull of endlessly intense work days and nights in the crazed weeks that followed, I asked John how it felt to be in the crosshairs of an educational assassination.

Silence grew as we tried to imagine what that meant.

It took no time to find out.

Informative Years

My initial act of political survival occurred spontaneously with sectarian authority at twelve years old. I served a 5:00 A.M. mass in a convent in a suburb of San Francisco where my family lived.

In the chapel sacristy of a hulking, scary-looking, and rank Victorian building constructed in the late nineteenth century, I blearily watched a Benedictine priest who escaped from Hungary following the anticommunist uprising in 1956 layer on vestments.

Without removing wire-rimmed glasses from his chubby face, he attempted to pull a green silk embroidered chasuble over his head. The opening in the chasuble wasn't large enough to accommodate his head and his glasses, yet he continued to pull it on.

The sight was the funniest live thing I'd ever seen. Riddled with laughter, I ducked out to light the altar candles.

Sniggering, I burst onto the altar to encounter—perched resolutely apart from each other in dark oak pews—an embarrassment of lonely and gloomy female boarding students from wealthy European and South American families, a couple of wraith-like elderly nuns, and the mother superior of my school. The bleak tableau spiked my risibility.

Mother superior's expression coarsened when she realized that I was giggling on the altar. I would be the victim of indelible wrath.

The boarding students, two nuns, and mother superior knelt down without a whisper at the communion railing. I could sense mother superior's rage as I backed toward her holding a paten under the chins of the etiolated communicants.

The priest reached into the chalice for a host and mother superior's stone-cold, vengeance-filled face dissolved into a pool of reverent piousness. Whether out of nervousness or by some unconscious force, I brushed her tightly roped neck with the paten.

Mother superior's pale blue eyes popped wide open.

She never mentioned my behavior.

I played football at a new public high school. At fifteen, I was already six feet two and one half, only one hundred and forty-five pounds, and all sharp elbows and knees. Principal interest was social life and I was beside myself when my father resigned his job in San Francisco to establish a business in Southern California. I completed a subdued and disconnected senior year at a different high school.

A resolutely marginal student, I enrolled in community college, working during the school year as a liquor store clerk and summers and holidays on a Port of Long Beach wharf, bagging and stacking fifty- and hundred-pound bags of water softener salt on wooden pallets and loading them with a forklift onto truck trailers or boxcars. Upon graduation, I enrolled at San Jose State University (then college) because friends from high school in Northern California were enrolled there.

Chronically Mentally Ill in the Campus Community

One warm spring evening on the San Jose State campus, I attended a jam-packed and highly animated meeting of the newly formed Campus Community Improvement Association. Homeowners were in an uproar about the demographic transformation of the campus community. Aware the human fabric of my neighborhood changed radically, I was genuinely surprised to learn that during the previous twelve months, the State of California had placed 1,800 ex-state mental hospital patients into the neighborhood.

San Jose State relaxed *in loco parentis* policies in part because of the 60s generation's sometimes compelling and mercilessly annoying antiestablishment attitudes and beliefs. Approved off-campus student housing was eliminated and scores of large private boarding facilities were eerily vacant.

There was also a precipitous decline in fraternity and sorority membership due to attitudes about the Pan-Hellenic system. Behind windows where coeds occasionally tossed panties to boozed-up fraternity boys were now warehoused—in grinding psychotropic stupors—hundreds of ex-state mental hospital patients. Former San Jose State-approved boarding houses were anesthetized with them.

Governor Reagan—and many other governors—successfully outsourced the cost of their states' chronically mentally ill to the Social Security system through Supplemental Security Income benefits for the disabled. As the result of these opportunistic shifts in financial responsibility from the states to the federal government, the chronically mentally ill nationally now constitute approximately 25 percent of daily jail and prison populations and a major percentage of the homeless.

Seventy-four percent of all board and care homes for the mentally ill in Santa Clara County were located in the one-square mile area around San Jose State and the improvement association claimed that they negatively affected lives and property values.

A local television station's warning was purple:

> *If you are a citizen of San Jose and have not visited the areas between Santa Clara and Williams and First and Twenty-Fourth Streets, you should do so, but only in a locked car during the daylight hours and never alone. It is difficult to believe that some of these people, many of whom are from Agnews [state mental hospital] are allowed to wander the streets. Many of them are within a few blocks of San Jose State University. A co-ed walking home at night is taking a chance with her life.*[22]

One would readily assume ex-patients' proximity to thousands of students earning degrees in the helping professions—psychology, abnormal psychology, sociology, psychiatric nursing, social work, counseling, and recreational and occupational therapy and the like—created opportunity for firsthand experience with the people with whom the nascent human service professionals would someday dedicate their lives.

This assumption proved gallingly wrong and helps explain why mental health and social service systems continue to grievously fail the most vulnerably mentally ill in the United States.

Community of Communities

An unregenerate 1960s-type—with no academic or other qualifications—I determined to create a student-operated program providing personal contact with people who were confined most of their adult lives in state mental hospitals, advocating for mental health services, facilitating independent living outside board and care facilities, and confronting and ameliorating the suspicion, fear, and hostility of the campus community toward their new, unwanted, and sometimes-unwashed neighbors.

I breezily named the project Community of Communities (C of C) for Plato's concept of *communitas communitatum,* gleaned from a western philosophy survey course. Revenue-sharing funds controlled by the county were available to fund innovative programs, including one serving ex-state mental hospital patients. Congress had enacted revenue-sharing legislation as a mechanism to return federal tax dollars to the states.

I sought out department chairs whose students were seeking mental health and social service degrees. My proposal for students to receive credit for working with the mentally ill literally across the street from the campus was condescendingly dismissed. I thought the experience would be a leg up on their careers. The department chairs archly avowed that their students were not academically qualified.

I learned from interacting personally and extensively with chronically mentally ill persons that there is often an inverse relationship between mental health and social service training and actual time ever spent with them.

Mainstream mental health professionals largely supported the physical deinstitutionalization of the mentally ill, but few their social deinstitutionalization.

I established conclusively that one doesn't need mental health or social service training to interact meaningfully with the chronically mentally ill or members of any other institutional subgroup.

I spoke before church and community groups and called on mental health and social service agencies and organizations. The heads of some key agencies refused to meet with me, so I persuaded the Associated Students of San Jose State to sponsor a campus community mental health forum. Agency heads eagerly joined the public panel I chaired.

I responded to the County of Santa Clara request for proposals for projects considered for federal revenue-sharing funds. Applications were accepted in spring and recipients selected in summer. Living entirely on savings, I spent every waking hour meeting with anyone who might support funding.

While a San Jose State student, I worked as a cannery forklift driver, a carpenter, house painter, bellman, fine dining waiter, submarine sandwich maker, criminal justice and education research assistant, cement chimney fabricator, night manager of the student union, and voter-registration coordinator. My rent was $25 per month and food another $25. Despite living below the poverty line, I could not wait for funding that might never be approved and still meet my piddling expenses.

I invited myself to a meeting of the Santa Clara County Mental Health Association to make a pitch for C of C in a last-ditch hope that an advocacy organization for the mentally ill might contribute seed funds to the only project in the county trying to do something with nearly two thousand ex-state mental hospital patients abandoned in the campus community.

The agency board listened attentively, passionately agreed there was a compelling need for such visionary services, and adjourned the meeting without doing anything. It was the end of my full-time efforts to establish C of C.

Community of Communities felt doomed.

A man named George McCarthy stopped me in the hallway outside the meeting room. George, a marine who fought on Guadalcanal, had been a social worker at Agnews State Hospital in Santa Clara County. Following its closure, he founded the Community Companions program to assist chronically mentally ill people to live independently.

He asked what I was going to do.

Get a job.

George opened his wallet and handed me a $100 bill.

Two months of rent and food.

George's belief in my idealism rescued Community of Communities and transformed my life. We became colleagues and close friends, and I served on the Community Companions board for many years. Late that summer, C of C was approved for revenue-sharing funds by the county board of supervisors.

Every fall and spring in those years, to register for classes, thousands of students waited in never-ending lines that serpentined through the San Jose State campus. I spent seemingly endless days recruiting students trapped in registration lines. Antiestablishment attitudes at that time were often accompanied by a burning desire to do something about social problems, and in a few weeks, C of C had over two hundred participants.

Despite working with those who had chronic mental illness, no one at C of C engaged in therapeutic activities other than those evolving spontaneously from personal relationships that flowered among students and former mental hospital patients. We focused on human problems, not mental illnesses.

Transportation, clothing, movies from the public library, use of San Jose State University facilities, field trips, dances, music tutoring, money management, ice cream socials, field days, a softball team—the *Organic All Stars*—made up of students and ex-state hospital patients. We would have beaten a San Jose police department team, but I let everyone play. Our weekly *Street Journal* itemized free events and services. We provided everything from dental hygiene classes to obtaining public benefits to facilitate transition into independent living.

I helped found the advocacy group, Parents of Adult Mentally Ill (PAMI), an association of the families of the ex-state mental hospital patients. Whether they liked it or not, families were the only constant in their lives. I subsequently published a layperson's guide to the mental health system. The *Family Journal of Mental Health* supported the creation of family advocacy groups for those with chronic mental illness throughout California. San Jose State New College film professor James Zuur made a documentary of the C of C project that is in the film archive of the California Department of Health. The California Association for Mental Health gave me an award for outstanding service.

The County of Santa Clara evaluated C of C. After a three-year evaluation, it was determined that the attitudes of the campus community toward the ex-state mental hospital patients fell from nearly 65 percent wanting them locked back up to a little more than 40 percent. Students entering ominous board and care homes and on neighborhood streets with sometimes scary looking and acting people contributed to the reduction of campus community fear and hostility.

When C of C began, 75 percent of the ex-state mental hospital patients were too frightened to go outside their board and care homes; three years later, it was 25 percent. The county executive recommended an additional year's funding.

To say the board of supervisors were gobsmacked when I turned down renewed funding is akin to the reaction a cardinal would generate from mumbling, "God is dead," at a Vatican synod.

I was fighting to convince the California legislature that the University of Phoenix was an academically legitimate and valuable asset to working adults, and Assembly Member Dan McCorquodale, a county supervisor when I turned down C of C funding, colorfully recalled what he still considered to be an out-of-body political experience.

I was the only director of a mental health or social service program who ever refused funding because the program no longer provided the quality it had once delivered—or for that matter—any other reason.

Spontaneous dedication of most C of C students had deteriorated during the previous year. During the first two years, virtually every student became personally committed to working with the chronically mentally ill, for many a difficult emotional and psychological transition. Many students in C of C's final year seemed primarily interested in the credits they could earn for participating in the program from the community mental health course I taught—after I earned my bachelors degree—as an adjunct faculty member at San Jose State and San Jose Community College.

The straw that broke the camel's back resulted from fundraising in which C of C students persuaded local businesses to donate to an auction. Students rigged the event to acquire the best items at stunted prices. So many were complicit, I was at a loss to repair the problem. Residents of board and care homes faced enough challenges without the burden of raised expectations now only with a marginal chance of being met.

The 1960s social conscience I had positively exploited had darkened convincingly.

It was time to move on.

CHAPTER

2

Crucible of Survival

Five months after I shuttered my community mental health project, I went to work as a political affairs consultant for University of Phoenix's predecessor and later sister company, the Institute for Professional Development (IPD), and reported to its president, John Sperling. John hired me because of Community of Communities.

Sperling and two of his former students founded IPD subsequent to John's meeting with the academic vice president of San Jose State. John reported on the successful field-testing of an off-campus degree program for working adults and wanted to institutionalize the prototype. John was reminded it needed to be approved by faculty committees, the faculty senate, and the chancellor's office of the California state university system.

It would take years.

Academic bureaucracy blocking innovation is a tried-and-true story, but John Sperling faced a barrier of his own devices at San Jose State. The year Martin Luther King and Bobby Kennedy were assassinated, Sperling, head of the American Federation of Teachers' (AFT) local, led a walkout in sympathy with a faculty strike at San Francisco State.

> *It was not a glorious action; only one-fourth of the membership participated, which left us with 100 professors and an equal number of student sympathizers walking around in the January rain for 31 days. Not only did I lose my credibility as a leader, I became the most disliked, often hated man on campus.*[23]

I did not know John Sperling, but did recognize him. Toward what proved to be the end of the walkout, I crossed a street that ran through the center of campus and was stopped in my tracks by the sight of an odd clutch of older men—including Sperling—penned within the stakes of a flatbed truck like bachelor farmers on the way to a county fair.

They were tepidly mangling the usually inspirational union song: *Solidarity Forever.*

They had already lost.

When Sperling field-tested the off-campus prototype, he repeatedly involved fellow professors. Few shared his work habits and most had distaste for dirtying their hands through the raw process of applying one's ideals. I was a social services entrepreneur who successfully implemented a campus-community-based program that had measurable results. We shared the same work ethic and were passionate about applying our beliefs in the real world.

It was a go.

Institute for Professional Development

The Institute for Professional Development (IPD) provides seed and operating capital to private liberal arts higher education institutions and assists them in the design and delivery of off-campus degree programs for working adults. Colleges bear virtually no financial risk, but if the extended degree programs prove successful, they split the tuition revenue; should programs fail, IPD takes the financial loss and the blame.

Despite declining enrollments among eighteen-to-twenty-four-year-olds that began in the 1960s and continued through 1990, hundreds and hundreds of private liberal arts colleges and universities in the United States closed because they were incapable or unwilling to survive through innovation, or were discouraged or prevented from doing so by their accrediting associations.

Resistance to innovation—other than mostly narrowly defined boutique-style, usually one-off programs—is a morbid conceit among some in traditional higher education and helps explain why many institutions and the associations that accredit them remain geologic in meeting the emerging educational needs of a rapidly evolving and increasingly sophisticated global economy in nontraditional ways, yet demand annual increases in degree costs considerably above the inflation rate.

Unwillingness to survive through innovation is rooted in obeisance to the orthodoxy of traditional higher education. Closure of many traditional private institutions can be traced to the adamantine belief that higher education is best provided one way: on a campus with full-time students and faculty, between certain months of the year, and commonly during the day.

This orthodoxy is fearsome.

Rather than innovate, survive, and preserve vital aspects of traditional institutions founded in the early twentieth century, some of the more than 2,500 private colleges and universities in the United States that ceased existence in the latter part of the twentieth century chose—or were forced to choose due to rigid accreditation standards—what was tantamount to institutional euthanasia.

There were once more private higher education institutions than public ones. Today, the opposite is true and America is paying a very high price because they are tax-supported. The costs of higher education rise ruthlessly each year and its critical role in supporting and preserving economic health and transmission of the culture remains under grave assault.

IPD Contracts

Following John Sperling's extended degree program pitch at San Jose State, he met with Frank Newman, a nationally regarded higher education visionary who was vice president for development at Stanford University.

John summarized Newman's response to his off-campus prototype:

> *(Y)ou'll never get a public institution to accept a truly innovative program. . . . The same thing is true for private institutions, especially if they consider themselves to be elite institutions. In fact, no institution that is financially healthy, including all public and private institutions, will innovate—they don't have to. Educational bureaucracies are dedicated to the status quo, and the only time they innovate is when they have to. The primary spur to financial*

innovation is financial necessity. What you need to do is find a school in financial trouble and convince the people running it that your adult education program will generate profit beyond the cost of the program.[24]

Traditional higher educators may blanch at the specter of financially vulnerable private institutions apparently importuned by a for-profit company to accept innovation in exchange for survival. Every college or university that entered IPD contracts needed to increase enrollment or face closure, yet arguably, not one would have acted had not IPD provided the capital.

Few traditional academics will risk a flat penny on innovation if it might even remotely affect the established order.

University of San Francisco, St. Mary's College, and the University of Redlands, California liberal arts institutions facing closure because of declining numbers of traditional-aged students, entered contracts with IPD to develop off-campus programs for working adults as the operative mechanism to save their institutions from closure.

Off-campus programs provided with the assistance of IPD were an immediate success in testimony to working adults' need for degree programs that acknowledged and accommodated the demands and responsibilities of working adulthood. The earthy response also revealed how higher education actually functioned in the marketplace.

Off-campus degree education without regard to putative market share inflamed the ire of some California academic traditionalists.

The first indication of trouble came when the administrators of competing institutions began to denounce the quality of IPD programs and to claim

> *that IPD was turning . . . [contract institutions] into . . . diploma mill(s).*[25]

Sperling placed the criticism of IPD and later the University of Phoenix into a historical context.

> *The battles fought by IPD and [University of Phoenix] against the educational establishment were, in a formal sense, regulatory battles, but they were larger proxies for cultural battles between defenders of 800 years of educational (largely religious) tradition, and an innovation that was based on the values of the marketplace—transparency, efficiency, productivity and accountability.*[26]

IPD's success also demystified how some contract school faculty and staff rhapsodized their place in higher education and, annoyingly, often interfered with their snug order of doing things. Some were even green-eyed that higher education capitalists identified a student demographic that responded enthusiastically to educational programs that allowed them to earn degrees while they worked full time.

IPD also snatched whatever change-agent thunder may have existed on contract campuses by pioneering substantive innovations that authentically met the educational needs of working adults. Many who decried the IPD innovations that ensured the survival of the institutions that employed them took less than self-effacing credit for those innovations once they had politically leveraged IPD out of the picture.

Another factor was the stunning response of the marketplace to completing one's degree while working full time. Rather than recognizing the legitimacy of working adults earning degrees off-campus, that IPD recruited large numbers of adult students was often perceived on contract campuses as the disease rather than the cure.

Some traditional academics nonchalantly sling the "diploma mill" slur to characterize colleges and universities that bring education to the consumer.

It's the academic diva syndrome: "We don't go to students; students come to us."

Many contract school administrators, faculty, and staff—and counterparts at other traditional institutions—were viscerally sickened when IPD used print and electronic media to recruit working adult students. Such practices were equated with advertising on matchbooks for degrees in art and private detective credentials, and splendidly justified the diploma mill label. Thousands of working adults attended information meetings to learn how off-campus degree programs could meet their educational, career, and lifestyle needs.

The advertising and information-meeting strategy was entirely practical. Most working adults had been in the workforce for years. Few had contact with higher education institutions for one reason; they would have to quit work to earn a degree. Peer awareness might play a critical role in the choice of a college or university when one is eighteen, but when one is thirty-six, peers either have earned degrees or are in the same boat.

Redefining the Postsecondary Education Marketplace

IPD educated the private liberal arts college marketplace on how degree programs designed to meet a working adult's learning needs differed from traditional on-campus programs.

What many exasperated full-time working adults knew about traditional degree programs is that after working an eight-hour day, they commuted usually three times a week to a campus, found parking, sat in a classroom with eighteen-to-twenty-four-year-olds with whom they had little in common, and listened passively to lectures focused on theory over three and a half months if on the semester system or a shorter amount of time if on the quarter system.

In IPD-assisted programs, they paid tuition and fees in class, with textbooks and other materials delivered the first night of each course. Rather than with younger students with whom they shared little, they were in small classes—twelve to eighteen students—with people their age, possessing similar real-world experience. The teaching/learning model required them to participate actively rather than listen passively.

Instead of being taught by academics theoretically familiar with the workaday world, they were instructed by working professionals with advanced degrees and at least five years' experience related to the courses they were teaching. Applied learning has marginal relevance to eighteen-to-twenty-four-year-old students without work or postsecondary academic experience, but was manifestly appropriate for midcareer working adults.

Classrooms were in proximity to where adult students lived and worked. Instead of taking one or two courses a semester or quarter, they took sequential five or six week courses that required attendance one night a week for four hours and a weekly meeting with a three-to-five-person study group. Rather than commencing degree programs in the fall or spring, they could begin any month of the year and complete courses sequentially until academic requirements were satisfied.

Diploma mill grumblings at contract school campuses were not uncommonly grief-stricken responses to performing routine tasks in real-world time. Accustomed at times to a somnambulant campus life, some staff and faculty reacted with alarm and resentment to having to process students for admission not once a semester, but each month of the year. Central to meeting needs of working adults was the elimination of the artifice of fall and spring enrollment.

Another source of painful affliction was the IPD recognition of working adults as informed consumers. Many faculty and staff became exercised when confronted by world-wise adult students demanding to know their admission status, complaining about course content or instruction, or demanding a grade to get tuition reimbursed by an employer.

Reaffirmation of accreditation at traditional institutions typically occurs every ten years and has marginal visibility and impact. Smaller, private, innovative institutions are most vulnerable to the power of accrediting associations because members of evaluation teams are usually from traditional institutions that constitute the largest segment of its membership. Institutions contemplating innovation are usually subject to "substantive change" provisions of the accrediting associations. In addition to faculty approval, proposals in this category are usually required to be approved prior to implementation by the accrediting association.

It is time-consuming, expensive, and exceedingly stressful if essential for survival.

Private nongovernmental accrediting associations are self-perpetuating. Members of their boards and commissions are ordinarily selected from among persons affiliated with the institutions they accredit, as are the evaluation teams. They voluntarily observe public sector reporting and access rules, and are not required to disclose personalized information on internal operations, board and evaluation team-selection processes, decision making, or the outcomes of any decision. Nongovernmental, private, voluntary associations, they are rarely victims of successful legal challenges.

These standards and values still dominate the way higher education is provided, despite that more than half of undergraduate students today are over twenty-five and work full or part time. The traditional structure of higher education, due to punishing annual cost increases and impediments to working-adult productivity must be changed to reflect the world in the twenty-first century rather than still operating like it was the late nineteenth century.

Higher Education Blasphemy

In response to the Western Association of Schools and Colleges (WASC) hounding—due to competitor and faculty complaints—of the three California IPD contract schools it accredited, John Sperling tasked me with pushing a bill through the California legislature to ameliorate its monopoly on the practice of higher education.

High profile political action by a for-profit higher education enterprise was received as a contemptible outrage by the California higher education establishment and was the foundation for enduring legislative and public-relations hostilities later encountered by the University of Phoenix.

This hard political action was undertaken because it was clear that no middle ground or compromise would be reached with WASC. Members of WASC teams evaluating IPD contract programs were often hostile, many times indifferent to fact or reason, and as John Sperling once observed, regularly acted like the Red Queen in *Alice in Wonderland*: first the verdict, then the evidence.

What was perceived as outrageously confrontational was an unquestionably rational response by higher education innovators exercising the hard political will necessary to protect their innovations. WASC appeared to have more regard for its capital-intensive accreditation standards than meeting the documented needs of California working adults for degree programs accommodating their learning needs and its importance to both the economy and society. Contract programs would hardly be evaluated in observance of dispassionate, objective, academic inquiry.

IPD was for profit and its tax status largely disqualified it from unbiased examination.

An outlier in the mental health and social service systems, I had little self-doubt about taking on the California higher education establishment. It was a supremely challenging fight and, most importantly, a legitimate political struggle over the critical value and importance of off-campus higher education for American working adults.

IPD Legislation

John Sperling had political and personal relationships with union members and their leaders. One, Mervyn Dymally, a former teacher, was lieutenant governor of California. Prompted by WASC denial of accreditation candidacy to an African American college in South Central Los Angeles, legislation challenging WASC's absolute authority had been introduced previously in the California legislature with Dymally's political support.

A freshman member of the assembly introduced an IPD bill at Dymally's request to establish public meeting standards and an independent appeals process for WASC. Still memorable from my first visit with the greenhorn representative in his capitol office was the sign on his desk: *You can lead a legislator to water and they will drink it.*

I saw an equally illuminating sign on another legislator's wall: *Old Age and Treachery Overcome Youth and Integrity.*

The IPD bill was heard in the Assembly Permanent Postsecondary Education Subcommittee in a temporary meeting room where its members were jammed together at a small rectangular table. Squeezing in tightly next to a long-serving Republican from the California central valley, IPD's champion fired up a cigarette.

The senior member of the committee crowded against him, face and neck incarnadine, asked him to not smoke. He took a deep drag, blew a gigantic nimbus, and the white-haired legislator stormed out.

IPD's bill didn't get out of the subcommittee.

Assembly Member John Vasconcellos, chair of the postsecondary education committee whom Sperling and I knew personally from San Jose State, had previously authored a bill to impose public meeting requirements on WASC. The political hook in the bill was that the lion's share of membership dues paid to WASC by its accredited institutions—based on numbers of students and campuses—was from taxpayers, because it came from California's community college, state university, and University of California systems.

Vasconcellos's bill passed the Assembly Education Committee and was scheduled for a Senate Education Committee hearing. The California Postsecondary

Education Commission, California State University, University of California, California Community Colleges, California State University faculty association, Association of Independent California Colleges and Universities, and WASC commenced a full-court political press against the bill.

The bill was held over for "interim study," the burial ground for controversial legislation. The opposition list remained intact to oppose all subsequent University of Phoenix California legislative efforts.

FBI at the Door

John Sperling and IPD then came hard against the coiled resentment of the California higher education establishment.

> *FBI agent[s] . . . descended on the IPD office in San Jose to examine an anonymous allegation that I [John Sperling] was guilty of a criminal conspiracy. The charges were no more specific than that I had somehow bribed officials at the University of San Francisco to gain their support for the IPD contract. They also claimed that I had bribed the Lieutenant Governor of California to induce him to support legislation that would strip WASC of its authority to accredit California colleges and universities. To substantiate the allegation, they sought evidence that I had siphoned money from IPD and had made cash payments to the Lieutenant Governor and a variety of John Does. Fully expecting to obtain evidence of my malfeasance from disaffected staff members, they systematically interrogated every employee who handled money, from tuition collection to the payment of vendors and*

> *staff salaries. When this produced no incriminating evidence, they brought in clerks to examine every check IPD had ever written. Again, there was no evidence.*[27]

Two FBI agents grilled me about Sperling's alleged illegal payment to the lieutenant governor. I had no knowledge or awareness of any such payment and, given my embarrassing and demoralizing experience with the IPD bill, observed something to the effect that relying on the lieutenant governor for political influence would be like relying on Mahatma Gandhi as a character reference for membership in the National Rifle Association.

Among selected IPD employees, I was flown to Los Angeles to be questioned under oath in front of a federal grand jury.

We were all sent home without testifying.

Under the federal Freedom of Information Act, John Sperling received a copy of the IPD FBI file with every name and date blacked out.

CHAPTER

3

Phoenix Ascendant

The University of Phoenix emerged from an Institute for Professional Development (IPD) contract with St. Mary's College, founded in the nineteenth century by the De La Salle Christian Brothers in Moraga, California, a suburban village east of Oakland. Like the University of San Francisco (USF) and the University of Redlands (Redlands) with whom IPD also held contracts, St. Mary's experienced a steady decline in traditional-aged students; student census needed to increase or it faced closure.

USF and Redlands were in similar straits and that was why, along with risking virtually nothing financially, all three entered IPD contracts.

IPD educated these institutions that working adults constituted a steadily increasing percentage of higher education enrollments. It proved difficult to get private liberal arts schools to respond to this demographic shift in the manner required to meet the educational needs of working adults. The delivery platform was alien to anything the institutions had ever experienced, and the most politically and philosophically difficult obstacles were accreditation standards and faculty approval.

Interpretation and application of accrediting standards of regional accrediting associations—particularly WASC and with the exception of the North Central Association—rarely resulted in the accreditation of stand-alone nontraditional higher education institutions for working adults. The development and implementation of off-campus programs for working adults was expensive, lengthy, and complicated under accrediting associations' substantive-change rules and the institutions' academic governance systems. The standard controlling change at traditional institutions is faculty approval.

Faculties at traditional institutions are storied for annihilating innovation.

Each California contract institution faced the necessity of increasing enrollment, but they had little idea how to deliver education off campus; what degree programs to offer or what course content; what teaching/learning model would meet the educational needs of older students who worked full time; how to recruit them; or how to incorporate nontraditional programs into the existing academic order.

Phoenix

IPD market research determined there were a significant number of working adults who completed some college in Phoenix, Arizona, and there were no off-campus degree programs offered by any Arizona public or private college or university. IPD established a St. Mary's extension office in downtown Phoenix and within a year, nearly three hundred Arizona working adult students were enrolled.

Working adults seeking degrees prior to St. Mary's off-campus programs were forced to drive two to three times a week to a community college or all or part way across Phoenix to Arizona State University in Tempe: 98.3 percent of Arizona college students then enrolled in tax-supported colleges and universities.

Traditional higher education remains structured and operated primarily for younger students who attend full time at a single campus. This compels working adults to earn degrees in a manner that can consume a decade during the most productive years of their lives. The negative impact on careers and on the economy is staggering. High percentages of working adults, who stop seeking degrees because of work, marriage, children, military service, or personal reasons, never return as full-time students. They spend years taking one course a semester or quarter. About half the time, they abandon their goal of earning a degree.

Average time-to-degree at traditional institutions is six plus years for students who attend full time. Families and individuals saving for and investing in a college education can also add annual increases in tuition and fees at up to five times the rate of inflation. Working adults also suffer the lost opportunity cost of the earnings differential between the college graduate and non-college graduate.

The majority of higher education institutions operate traditionally, although many have made allowances for working adults through weekend and online courses and satellite campuses. Some traditional academicians are wont to appear on the cutting edge of change and deftly wield the argot of innovation to colorize what remain blandly conventional practices. Based on the observance of an agrarian calendar established in the late nineteenth century, most traditional institutions provide the bulk of educational services between September and May.

The Carnegie Unit pedagogical model established in the early twentieth century—as a faculty pension structure—remains the teaching/learning paradigm at traditional institutions in the twenty-first century. For each credit, a student allegedly expends fifteen hours in the classroom and studying. There is sometimes a weighty disconnection between seat time and learning. Few, if any, institutions document attendance or assess, independent of the instructor, whether students actually learned anything.

The Carnegie Unit algorithm is lucrative because traditional colleges and universities calculate tuition and fees against it. Some respond fiercely to its breach lest it be discovered that it is not essential for educational quality or academic success. Campus-based education is capital-intensive, and most regional and programmatic accrediting associations reflect that metric in the interpretation of standards and operating rules.

A preeminent article of faith among many traditional academics is that higher education is never provided at a profit, yet it was those from this high-minded milieu the University of Phoenix sought to evaluate and accredit its for-profit, nontraditional approach to the education of working adults.

Higher education, despite its reach and effect on the lives of tens of millions of Americans, remains an insular part of American society. This becomes painfully clear when attempts are made to institutionalize innovations that, by design and practice, defy time-honored academic standards.

The University of Phoenix accepted that to be a legitimate higher education institution, it had to earn accreditation. Regional accrediting agencies are controlled by academics from traditional colleges and universities, and the accreditation process was inherently onerous, sometimes prejudicial, demanded extraordinary attention to detail, and was a political minefield.

For my entire tenure, virtually nothing described or claimed by the University of Phoenix was ever taken at face value by accrediting associations, accredited colleges and universities, state licensing agencies, state legislatures, employers, potential students, or the media. All felt compelled to repeatedly verify University of Phoenix's academic, administrative, and financial operations.

A not insignificant portion of the responsibility for inherent skepticism and sometimes hostility was of our own invention. Traditional higher education didn't seek out the University of Phoenix; we sought it out. We required accreditation to be recognized by accredited institutions for both the transfer of credit and degree recognition, employers for hiring and educational reimbursement programs, and to qualify for federal and state student loans.

The for-profit corporate structure and nontraditional educational model was a radical departure from the values and beliefs that—in increasingly problematic ways because of annual cost increases in excess of the inflation rate—struggle to serve students, society, the economy, and the nation.

The University of Phoenix was a manifestly off-putting enigma to accreditation evaluators from traditional higher education:

- Classrooms anywhere,
- No campus, offices,
- No library, but electronic learning resources,
- Curriculum department authors courses,
- Instructors work full time in other professions,
- Working adult students complete courses sequentially and attend class four hours one night a week for five or six weeks,
- Credits awarded toward bachelor's degrees for college-level learning gained through experience,
- Degree programs start every month of the year, and
- Profit-making.

Get a bucket of cold water and perhaps a revolver.

St. Mary's/IPD off-campus program success in California and Arizona gradually eased its financial difficulties. Despite this critical achievement, WASC, St. Mary's accrediting association, after the University of Phoenix was granted candidacy for accreditation, threatened St. Mary's with loss of accreditation if it didn't stop offering degrees in Arizona and terminate its IPD contract.

WASC, like five other regional accrediting associations recognized by the Council on Postsecondary Accreditation, was mandated to evaluate institutions in light of their missions. This evaluation construct permits, encourages, and endorses innovation in recognition of changing student demographics and economic need. WASC and most other regional accrediting associations at the time—with the exception of North Central—required institutions to fit into a Procrustean bed of capital-intensive standards independent of their missions.

A campus, library, full-time faculty, and observance of the Carnegie Unit were usually absolutes.

WASC-approved IPD contracts with its accredited institutions and off-campus programs realized immediate success in affirmation of real-world need. Off-campus enrollment quickly outpaced and even outgrew campus enrollment. IPD earned a return on its investment and WASC hauntingly concluded that academic anarchy had been loosed by a for-profit enterprise responsible only to its owners.

> *The whole regulatory structure of higher education is designed to favor nonprofit and public colleges and universities. . . . (T)his difference in treatment represents a cultural prejudice that arose from centuries of practice. Beginning with the University of Bologna, founded in the twelfth century, down to Harvard College and its American offspring, ranging from large state universities to community colleges, to small church-related colleges, education for profit simply doesn't seem right; it violates the established order of things.*[28]

California colleges and universities with unchallenged places in the marketplace found themselves in competition with previously campus-bound IPD contract schools. They operated as virtual monopolies, but rather than meet the challenge, they accused IPD of turning the contract institutions into diploma mills. IPD contributed materially to the perception. It aggressively marketed degree programs because it was the practical way to reach adults who worked full time.

IPD financially stabilized all three of its California contract schools, but some on their campuses became opportunistic victims of WASC bullying. Dire imprecations about loss of accreditation clouded the issues, and willfully ignoring that IPD saved their institutions and their jobs, some faculty and staff clambered onto the academic ramparts and bawled that IPD had become the "tail that wagged the campus dog."

Sever the IPD tail or their institutions would become diploma mills!

William Umbach, a University of Redlands dean who supported IPD, compared the treatment of IPD by faculty and staff once their institutions had been rescued from financial demise to the treatment of the title character in Guy de Maupassant's short story, "*Boule de Suif* (Butterball)."[29]

Butterball—a patriotic French prostitute—was convinced by a tidy group of wealthy citizens and a couple of nuns held captive by an advance company of an invading Prussian army to sleep with an enemy officer so that they could be freed. Following her sacrifice and their freedom, they cruelly shunned her. The "Butterball Effect" manifested with a number of IPD contract institutions. (See Appendix I: *The Butterball Effect*, p. 245.)

CHAPTER

4

Creation of The University of Phoenix

Facing the real probability of California IPD contracts being terminated and certainly not renewed, and confronted with the political maintenance of an increasingly fractious, sometimes aggressively hostile California contract college faculty and staff, John Sperling determined to create a university designed and operated solely to meet educational needs of full-time working adults.

St. Mary's agreed to an educational consortium to facilitate University of Phoenix evaluation for accreditation in Arizona, and application for candidate for accreditation was submitted to the Commission of Institutions of Higher Education—now Higher Learning Commission—of the North Central Association of Colleges and Schools, the regional accrediting entity for Arizona and eighteen other states.

Initially the new higher education institution was named the Institute for Professional Development. To avoid confusion with the IPD consulting company, it was later renamed University of Phoenix for the city in which it was founded.

Valley of the Sun's powers-that-be, particularly the "Phoenix Forty," an association of civic and business movers and shakers, were outraged that some California for-profit academic carpetbaggers swiped the name of Arizona's flagship city for a private university. Resentment stewing prior to the maiden *Arizona Republic* diploma mill article gave currency to negative public opinion and added political horsepower to the Arizona regents' subsequent efforts to put the University of Phoenix out of business by seizing control of the state licensure of private colleges and universities.

Dr. Peter Ellis, a co-founder and shareholder of IPD, was openly critical of John Sperling's creation of the University of Phoenix. When they founded IPD, Sperling convinced Ellis of the necessity—allegedly to prevent decision gridlock and in recognition of John's academic pedigree as the holder of a Cambridge University doctorate—of one shareholder holding majority ownership; John that shareholder.

Sperling controlled 60 percent of the stock, Ellis and other shareholder Carole Crawford, 20 percent each. John didn't need anyone's vote to make a decision. Ellis appeared to have made an irreversible blunder when, in the face of stupendously calamitous academic and political opposition to the University of Phoenix, he couldn't prevent John from continuing to invest riskily limited IPD financial resources in it.

Ellis was bowled over when North Central granted candidacy for accreditation, but any glow faded almost immediately. Only a month after the labeling of the University of Phoenix as a diploma mill in the Arizona news media, it faced challenges spectacularly out of scale to its size and limited time in existence.

If we failed to overcome even one of them, the University of Phoenix was a goner.

- The *Arizona Republic* diploma mill article had been orchestrated by the Arizona Board of Regents and created a lethal public relations and economic problem: no students would enroll.
- The Arizona state university system engaged in sustained political efforts with North Central to block the accreditation of the University of Phoenix.
- The Arizona regents introduced legislation to seize control of the licensure of private higher education. The public diploma mill controversy identified with the University of Phoenix was intended to bulldoze its passage.
- The legislation would provide regents the authority to deny University of Phoenix licensure and we were forced to expend exceedingly limited financial resources to prevent its enactment.
- Without an Arizona state license, the University of Phoenix would be automatically disqualified as a candidate for North Central accreditation.
- Toxicity of the University of Phoenix's public image and legislative threat to licensure forced the request of an evaluation for accreditation the second year of candidacy rather than the customary fifth year.

- If legislation was defeated and the accreditation evaluation team recommended continued candidacy—a likely outcome given our limited time in existence—the University of Phoenix would perish because no students would enroll: "Wait until you're accredited."
- Funding was derived solely from profits generated by IPD. When the University of Phoenix was granted candidacy, WASC, which accredited all three of California contract institutions—IPD's only contracts—threatened loss of accreditation if those contracts weren't terminated.
- Toxic public relations; predatory legislation; long odds against being granted accreditation in the second year of candidacy; political interference with accreditation evaluation, and loss of accreditation threats to IPD's only contract institutions unearthed increasingly toxic antipathies between Peter Ellis and John Sperling.

Welcome to the Grand Canyon state.

With eight students, the impossibility of recruiting new students until accredited, and deadly threats about loss of accreditation to California contract institutions, a full-court press was undertaken to generate contracts with private colleges and universities across the country. If new revenue sources were not secured, IPD and the University of Phoenix would perish. John Sperling recounted the results of visiting fifteen private colleges and universities.

> *The . . . institutions with which we negotiated contracts all proved to be stopgap measures. At Lesley*

> *College (Cambridge, MA), we only had a marketing consulting contract that provided very little positive cash flow. The Elmhurst College (Elmhurst, Illinois), was given only lukewarm support by the college administration, was marginally profitable, and lasted only three years. The National College of Education (Evanston, IL) was enthusiastically supported by the administration, but the problem was collecting IPD's share of the revenue.*[30]

St. Mary's/University of Phoenix Consortium

North Central granted candidacy to the University of Phoenix in part because the consortium permitted inclusion of St. Mary's Phoenix operation into its evaluation for accreditation.

The consortium with St. Mary's was deemed appropriate by North Central because curricular design and content, its teaching/learning model, faculty training, administrative structure and services, and financial and academic management systems in the St. Mary's Phoenix programs were identical to those of the University of Phoenix. For purposes of evaluation for accreditation, St. Mary's Phoenix students and faculty were considered University of Phoenix students and faculty.

As the consequence of continuing diploma mill stories—others had appeared in the *Phoenix Gazette*, Arizona State, University of Arizona, and Tucson newspapers, as well as similar reports in the broadcast media—and despite persistent efforts, for the year following the inaugural diploma mill article, not one student enrolled at the University of Phoenix.

Today, the University of Phoenix is one of the largest private accredited higher education institutions in the world. Numbers of students often represent everything many need to know about any college or university.

There are good reasons for the statistical credibility of the University of Phoenix: 700,000 graduates, a hundred some campuses from coast to coast, and over 300,000 students enrolled. In states where the University of Phoenix has campuses, everybody seems to know someone who attends, attended, or graduated. Where there are offices and classrooms, it is not uncommon for a freeway sign to point the way.

There is a much more complex and revealing story behind the success of the University of Phoenix: the life and death struggle against implacable and sometimes underhanded opposition by traditional academics and their regulatory, policy, legislative, and media allies and minions.

Opposition continued unabated despite that at one point, accreditation teams were composed of representatives of more than half of the six regional accrediting associations in the United States. Only when it came to the University of Phoenix did some traditional academics fail to acknowledge the probity of their peers' evaluation findings—verified repeatedly through on-site visits—as to the quality of its education for working adults.

The high-profile success of the University of Phoenix is both admired and reviled, but the real story lies in the Herculean struggle to create, refine, and institutionalize cutting edge and enduring educational innovations to serve working adult learners, and the diligence of the hard political will necessary to protect and defend those efforts.

The University of Phoenix was once the undisputed gold standard in nontraditional higher education for working adults, not only because of the substantive quality of its educational innovations, practices, and academic content, but also because traditional higher education—with limited concessions to the adult learner—continues to function primarily in the same centralized, capital-intensive manner in which it has operated historically.

There isn't much competition because most traditional institutions fail to acknowledge the educational needs of working adult students as authentic by materially changing the academic architecture by which they provide degree education.

Educational change is often philosophical confetti at traditional institutions because it is rarely accompanied by the enthusiasm to dirty one's hands by fighting for it politically. Absence of hard political will results in crib deaths of untold and sometimes valuable educational innovations. Successful innovation is tied inextricably to the hard willingness and skill of its innovators to defend it, regardless of the form of the opposition or obstacles in its path.

Real change is a challenge to the existing order: if it doesn't challenge the existing order, it is not authentic change. Traditional higher education has elaborate structures and processes to ensure its monopoly remains intact. Many in higher education who posture themselves as visionaries and change agents simply fail to engage in or duck engaging in the often bare-knuckled political fights necessary to bring envisioned changes to term.

Regardless of origin or form of attacks, we worked unrelentingly to meet each challenge, solve every problem, and address all failures. Despite overwhelming odds against our very survival, we daily kept our noses to the grindstone. We labored ceaselessly to improve all aspects of the University of Phoenix and communicate the precise nature of our innovative teaching/learning model for working adults to the public, employers, the media, regulatory and accreditation agencies, politicians, and state and federal regulators.

A higher education institution of the likes no one had much seen, much less understood, it was easy for facile detractors to trade on the diploma mill slur, particularly when the representatives of high-profile, well-regarded higher education systems, institutions, and organizations employed it publicly and privately.

The academic slur, *diploma (or degree) mill,* commonly refers to entities that award degrees without the requirement of learning in exchange for payment, but for many University of Phoenix detractors, it is the code cliché for for-profit education. Despite being accredited and having accreditation reaffirmed repeatedly for more than thirty-five years, because the University of Phoenix remains for-profit, it will always be dismissed by many traditional academics as a diploma mill.

Faced with sometimes irrational, often overtly hostile attitudes that gave rise to media attacks and legislative initiatives, the singular choice was to tell the truth; answer all questions candidly and comprehensively; never exaggerate or embellish facts; work determinedly to accurately define and describe the educational philosophy, structure, and practices of the University of Phoenix so that misconception and mischaracterization were minimized; and bear absolute accountability for student academic achievement.

A factor that undermined efforts to communicate the elements of an unconventional educational model was the use of the nomenclature of accredited nontraditional education by diploma mills—profiled in a CBS *60 Minutes* expose—that held licenses issued by the California Office of Private Postsecondary Education. These ersatz educational operations plagiarized the terminology employed by legitimate nontraditional institutions to describe academic processes that resulted in the award of degrees without education.

Unaccredited colleges and universities licensed by California as academic degree-granting institutions often marketed themselves as nontraditional institutions for working professionals. Nothing more than a narrative of "life experiences" and a few thousand dollars could result in the issuance of a terminal degree.

California's make-believe college credentials were attractive to foreign nationals who didn't know the difference between state licensure and accreditation, and among thousands of Americans who believed their school of hard knocks experiences should be celebrated with a terminal degree, even if they paid someone to print it.

The few traditional academics possessing knowledge of the California-licensed academic Potemkin villages were astonished when North Central granted candidacy for accreditation to an institution that, at least superficially, appeared to describe isolated aspects of its educational model in the same terms.

Repeated evaluations reaffirmed the quality of University of Phoenix educational model and academic offerings, but there remained those who refused to acknowledge the findings of their peers from the same bodies that accredited the institutions where they were employed. The diploma mill slur frees traditional academics from observing the scientific method of evaluation they profess to follow in their own disciplines and impart to their students. John Sperling once so noted in a communication to the Arizona

Board of Regents:

> *To me, the most disturbing aspect of the present situation is that the persons who provided the Regents with information concerning University of Phoenix, violated every tenet of scholarship that is the foundation of any university. Their allegations were not based on research, showed no respect for fact or sound argument, and were uttered with no concern for the harm which they certainly knew these allegations would cause.*[31]

Over its first twenty years, over two hundred independent senior academics and administrators from North Central and other regional accrediting associations conducted, variously, on-site evaluation visits, reviewed visiting team findings and recommendations, or affirmed the evaluation teams' and review committees' recommendations for reaffirmation of accreditation.

First in Arizona, then in California and other states, the diploma mill slur remained extant in the media and in the attitudes of many traditional academics ill disposed toward the University of Phoenix, regardless of the quality vetted repeatedly by teams of independent accreditation evaluators.

Without the often intimidating efforts of the Arizona state university system and others to corrupt North Central decision making, the University of Phoenix would not have been accredited in its second year of candidacy and grown into one of the largest private accredited higher education institutions in the world. Knocked down repeatedly by one sucker punch after another revealed the best in most of us. Often-hidebound academic opposition was a profoundly transformative factor in our success.

Opponents' behavior played catalytic roles in the granting of accreditation, the defeat of legislation that would place the licensure of private colleges and universities under the thumb of public higher education, the recognition of degrees and transfer credits, and the maintenance of accreditation reciprocity for purposes of state licensure.

Our enemies from traditional higher education made us infinitely stronger and more effective than if we had proceeded with no opposition.

The University of Phoenix would not exist today without them.

With the exception of the University of Phoenix and a limited number of other institutions for working adults, the majority of working adults struggle to complete their undergraduate degrees in a manner designed and operated for traditional-aged students.

The loss of personal and economic productivity because of their inability to earn a degree in a manner that complements their real-world responsibilities can never be recovered.

It is well beyond the time for comprehensive structural changes in the way higher education is conceived and delivered. The University of Phoenix was established closer to the twenty-first than twentieth century and both its design and operation acknowledge and reflect the time in which it was founded. The majority of America's traditional higher education institutions remain configured and managed as if we were at the turn of the nineteenth century.

In 1900, communication was measured in weeks, months, and even years; today, it's nanoseconds.

CHAPTER

5

Candidacy for Accreditation— Educational Model for Working Adults

A San Jose State colleague, a former member of the Arizona House of Representatives, put John Sperling in contact with the chief of staff of Arizona Governor Raoul Castro, Dino DeConcini. Dino is a scion of one of Arizona's prominent Democrat political families; his brother Dennis was an Arizona United States senator for many years. He linked Sperling to one of Arizona's most prominent and influential Republican law firms.

The firm recruited three highly regarded Arizonans as University of Phoenix board members. Ray Shaffer started as a bus driver at Greyhound and became its president. Dr. John Prince founded the Maricopa County, Arizona, community college district; attorney and prominent Democrat, William Mahoney, was JFK's ambassador to Ghana.

The choice to make the University of Phoenix for-profit was seditious for any higher education institution, much less a nontraditional one. It guaranteed the enmity of some from traditional higher education—the people who would evaluate the University of Phoenix for accreditation—but established credibility with working adults and employers who provide educational support as an employee benefit.

Working adults and their employers enjoy little direct accountability from tax-supported colleges and universities, but because the University of Phoenix was for-profit, they could and did hold it accountable for the quality of its education and the academic achievements of its students. This corporate tax status buoyed the University of Phoenix during some of its darkest and most defenseless hours.

The self-congratulatory assertion by WASC and other California higher education powers-that-be that they drove John Sperling and IPD out of California is more accurately attributed to an informed political management decision, given WASC behavior toward for-profit nontraditional higher education and its imposition of traditional capital-intensive academic standards on virtually all innovation.

WASC allowed traditional institutions to develop off-campus programs for working adults, but rarely recognized them as distinct learners for accreditation of a stand-alone nontraditional institution. Annual cost increases at highly capital-intensive traditional institutions make it financially onerous and increasingly impossible for most full-time working adults—and now even many traditional-aged students—to earn a college degree.

North Central was the premier change agent in institutional accreditation. In the early 1900s, accreditation standards specified the precise number of library books and square footage. North Central was the first regional accrediting association to recognize that such explicit standards narrowed the method and manner by which education could be provided, with a negative impact on creativity, diversity, and quality.

North Central was also the first to evaluate each institution in the context of its educational mission and purposes: is the institution materially achieving its legitimate and appropriate educational goals and objectives?

The national accreditation recognition body, the Council on Postsecondary Accreditation, made this a requirement for all regional accrediting associations. All, including WASC, adopted the principle. It allowed for the recognition of the working adult learner as a separate and distinct type of student.

Historically, traditional higher education has exhibited a congenital resistance to change. In the early twentieth century, private colleges and universities—once the majority of institutions—protested fiercely against the creation of tax-supported land-grant colleges and universities. Another pitched battle followed World War II when private and public higher education institutions fought the GI Bill because they believed it debased student quality.

One reason North Central exercised a primary leadership role in the evolution of institutional accreditation, in addition to experience tied to longevity because it is one of the two oldest accrediting associations in the United States, is because it is the largest regional accrediting association, encompassing nineteen states.

With over one thousand accredited colleges and universities, North Central rarely faced problems arising from refereeing market share among institutions. Members of its commission, board of directors, and evaluation teams are drawn from a vast pool of higher education professionals; few if any, possess conflict of interest problems with any institution being evaluated.

To help ensure that no conflict of interest compromises an accreditation decision, no individual from a college or university in the same state as the one evaluated was allowed to participate on the visiting team, the review committee evaluating the team's findings and recommendations, the commission approving or denying the recommendation or making a new recommendation, or its executive board.

WASC, whose geographical region encompassed California, Hawaii, Guam, Samoa, and the Pacific Trust Territories—virtually all of its accredited colleges and universities being California institutions—is the most ingrown of the six regional associations. With a relatively limited pool of individuals to perform evaluations and approve or deny the evaluation team's recommendations, WASC is also the most narrowly self-perpetuating; it had no geographic conflict in interest rule like North Central.

Evidenced by its heavy-handedness with IPD contract institutions, WASC apparently perceived nothing wrong with enforcing competitor institution judgment over a fellow institution. Competition for students by private colleges and universities was accelerated by an increasing shift in student demographics. In the 1970s, there were fewer eighteen-to-twenty-four-year-olds in the student pool.

The University of Phoenix was granted candidacy for accreditation and WASC immediately informed St. Mary's that its Arizona programs offered with the assistance of IPD would no longer be considered part of its accreditation. St. Mary's protested but there was no recourse for a quick resolution. Brother Dominic Ruegg, St. Mary's academic vice president, and John Sperling found a way out of the problem by changing the description from a consortium to "St. Mary's—IPD Cooperative Program."

Evaluation for Candidacy

Dr. Thurston Manning, a former professor of physics, executive director of the North Central Commission on Institutions of Higher Education, while open to the evaluation of a for-profit university for working adults, brooked no compromise in the administration of evaluation for candidacy for accreditation.

> *(T)he Chairman was Dr. Donald Roush, Academic Vice President of New Mexico State University; the two other members were Dr. Wade Ellis, Professor of Mathematics and Associate Dean of the Graduate School at the University of Michigan, Ann Arbor; and Dr. Roy Trout, President of the University for Sciences and the Arts of Oklahoma.*[32]

Team findings and recommendation for candidacy status were provided to a review committee and then to the North Central commission. Both affirmed candidacy.

Wade Ellis allowed that the concern about chances for candidacy was not ill founded. Ellis came to Phoenix to put a for-profit diploma mill out of existence, but determined the University of Phoenix was an authentic educational enterprise. Ellis's acknowledgment that he initially considered the University of Phoenix a diploma mill confirmed that efforts to politically compromise the accreditation evaluation had occurred even prior to candidacy.

In response to the review committee's recommendation that clarification needed to be made between the IPD consulting company and the IPD degree-granting institution, the IPD board changed the name of the Arizona IPD corporation to the University of Phoenix in recognition of the city in which it was founded and in acknowledgment of the metaphor of the mythical Phoenix arising from the ashes—working adults unable to earn degrees at traditional institutions. Even the name selection attracted intense controversy.

The enduring prejudice and hostility of the *Arizona Republic* and *Phoenix Gazette* toward the University of Phoenix had a short-lived but welcome respite.

Darrow "Duke" Tully, the publisher of both papers, proudly claimed for years to have flown a hundred sorties in Vietnam and prominently displayed a Purple Heart, Distinguished Flying Cross, and Vietnam Cross of Gallantry on a handsome dress Air Force colonel's uniform.

Tired of being pilloried in Tully's newspapers, the Maricopa County District Attorney was driven to discover that Tully had never served a day in the Air Force or any other branch of the military.

Tully high-tailed it out of Arizona.

"Duke" worked at the *San Francisco Examiner* during the IPD/WASC controversy.

Educational Model for Working Adults

At the core of the excoriation of everything University of Phoenix is the refusal of many traditional academics to acknowledge that full-time working adults require an educational delivery system and teaching/learning model designed and operated in recognition of their specific learning needs and place in life. Recognition of differences in educational delivery systems and teaching/learning models for the traditional-aged student with limited experience and the one for full-time working adults with real-world experience is the key to the transformation of undergraduate higher education in the twenty-first century.

Virtually all those who control higher education through accreditation work at traditional institutions. They commonly transmit and affirm its core beliefs and values in their evaluation of educational innovation and change. With the exception of the University of Phoenix, and other innovative private institutions and higher education institutions with satellite campuses and online courses, most working adult students are treated like traditional-aged students.

Because it liberates them from making substantive changes, some academics at traditional institutions expropriate the rubric of innovative higher education to describe conventional functions. Regional accreditation bodies like North Central evaluate institutions in light of the educational goals and objectives established to achieve their missions because it allows innovation to meet both changing demographic demands and needs of an evolving economy.

Regional accrediting bodies that fail to evaluate institutions in observation of national recognition criteria, but force narrow adherence to traditional standards, simply refuse to acknowledge that working adults require an educational delivery system different from that provided on campus to younger students.

The University of Phoenix teaching/learning model for working adults attracted legitimate and illegitimate criticism. Legitimate criticism was usually framed as the failure to honor traditional academic principles. The answer was the demonstration and documentation of the equivalency of educational outcomes.

Virtually every element of the adult learning model challenged the received order, but one reason we survived a highly politicized evaluation accreditation was fidelity to our mission. Despite sometimes-intense criticism in the context of ongoing media attacks, we refused to modify our educational model or tax structure.

It was our persevering resistance to change while seeking endorsement of change that ensured our survival.

There was virtually nothing about the educational model that didn't heighten apoplexy among traditional academics who persisted in being muddled as to its actual nature and operation. Some traditionalists made predictable recommendations: full-time faculty, faculty authorship of courses, single campus, observe the Carnegie Unit, become nonprofit, restrict the start of degree programs, eliminate college-level learning gained through experience, and modify administrative titles.

The University of Phoenix used nomenclature common to the management of for-profit enterprises.

Some evaluators believed if the University of Phoenix closely reflected conventional practices it would be readily welcomed into their exclusive club. We resisted conformance to the traditional, even though the distortions and misrepresentations of our teaching/learning model and mission found credibility with the public and potential working adult students.

We knew how to describe, defend, and validate the teaching/learning model. If we listened to those urging us to modify it, we would have been neither architects nor apologists for the modifications and, if and when things went south, those who made the recommendations would be nowhere to be found.

Refusal to modify the educational model despite relentless critical attacks provided the foundation for accreditation.

North Central teams conducting on-site evaluations and the commission verified that the teaching/learning model functioned as we documented it, rather than how our critics pigeonholed it. In this politicized context, if we succumbed to the siren calls to become traditional, our educational integrity would be in tatters, and the teaching/learning model would have been eliminated as one of the bases of our accreditation. It was steadfastness in adhering to our adult learning principles that helped ensure that our adult learning model was endorsed through accreditation.

North Central Replaces the University of Phoenix as Political Target

The integrity of our teaching/learning model stood in sharp relief because many critics at tax-supported institutions were addicted to their righteousness against a for-profit university. Given our unyielding commitment to our educational and corporate principles, the North Central Association soon replaced the University of Phoenix as the primary political target of the Arizona state university system.

Representatives of North Central—and the association itself—were accused of allowing the University of Phoenix to—de facto—buy its candidacy.

The challenge to the integrity of North Central helped ensure that the University of Phoenix became accredited in two years rather than five years. The challenge reflected little understanding of accreditation, but rather the hubris of some representatives of the Arizona tax-supported higher education system who behaved as if a private higher education institution and a prestigious regional accrediting body were accountable to no one but them.

The state university system largely ignored the learning needs of Arizona working adult students, but was intent on destroying the only entity that endeavored to do so. Its hostile position strengthened our credibility when Arizona employers informed us they had been struggling for years to get the state university system to develop off-campus programs that met the personal and professional needs of their workers, their companies, and the economy.

Prior to the University of Phoenix being granted candidacy for accreditation, John Sperling contacted the executive coordinator of the Arizona Board of Regents to introduce himself, identify the well-regarded Arizona members of the board of directors, explain the nature and operation of a higher education institution designed to meet the learning needs of Arizona adults who worked full time, and advise him of the application for North Central accreditation.

The executive coordinator personally assured John that any institution that sought North Central accreditation was welcome in Arizona.

John Sperling also met with the Arizona Superintendent of Public Instruction, Dean Weber of the Arizona State University (ASU) School of Education, Donald Bell, Executive Director of the Arizona Commission for Postsecondary Education, ASU President John Schwada, and ASU Vice Presidents Karl Dannenfeldt and Al Weaver to inform them of the application for candidacy and to explain the substance and nature of a nontraditional university solely for working adults.

Arizona Board of Regents, their staff, and three state universities dedicate a generous amount of time and effort to maintain and increase budget allocations. Almost without exception, tax dollars sought are defined as bricks and mortar and the salaries and benefits of faculty and staff. For most, new facilities, classrooms and laboratories, libraries, student housing, staff and faculty pension or health plans epitomized what higher education looked and felt like.

Most traditional college and university administrators and faculty know little about regional accreditation other than that about every ten years a campus committee is tasked with an institutional self-study. Using the self-study report, a visiting evaluation team roots through documents and interviews representative faculty, staff, and students. Virtually without exception, accreditation is reaffirmed for another ten years.

Those even aware of the evaluation for continued accreditation at large traditional institutions sometimes wonder—if they wonder at all—about its relevance.

The prism by which many at traditional colleges and universities view what is acceptable and unacceptable in higher education typically captures its capital-intensive components, and when that prism was used to look at the University of Phoenix, nothing was there.

Most critics possessed little understanding of the evaluation construct that required the judgment of each institution in light of the goals and objectives it had established for itself. It allows for a variety of educational missions, whether input-measured, capital-intensive standards appropriate for the young undergraduate student who attends full time on a single campus, or output-measured standards focused on learning demonstrated by the students in recognition of their maturity, experience, and status as full-time working adults.

The University of Phoenix failed to meet virtually every shop-worn traditional academic value on which conventional academicians had built their careers, and was therefore simply not a legitimate higher education institution.

Ipso facto, University of Phoenix candidacy for accreditation meant that North Central abandoned its standards.

Despite WASC and the Arizona state university system reaction to the University of Phoenix, recognized academic theory identified the differences between traditional-aged and working adult students. The principal catalyst of the critics' angst was the shift from the theoretical to the applied through the establishment of an institution dedicated solely to the working adult learner.

The University of Phoenix pioneered the delivery of higher education to working adults but embodied received principles of adult learning in almost everything it did.

> *University of Phoenix curricula rely less upon the transmittal techniques of the teaching paradigm employed with persons with a limited experience base, and more upon techniques, which call upon and evolve the previous experiences of the learners. The use of lectures, audio-visual presentations, and other passive learning activities is de-emphasized in favor of such small group activities as discussions, simulation, role playing, field experiences, and team projects.*[33]

Principles of this teaching/learning model are appropriate to meeting the learning needs of mature working adult students. In addition to homage paid to working adult learners, it honored received wisdom about professional obsolescence.

> *It has become clear that the dominating concept in education, i.e. the completion of a formal program in a prescribed number of years as adequate preparation for a lifetime of work, must give way to the concept of lifelong education as an integral part of an adult's career. University of Phoenix is committed to developing and evaluating programs which meet the professional needs of working adults who wish to stay current with the "state of the art" of their professions.*[34]

Despite withering criticism by some in the Arizona state university system, we were consonant with thinking on the transformation of higher education to meet the needs of a changing world.

> *The next three decades are likely to be a period of substantial innovation and change in the organizational structure of higher education. Along with the continuation of recent trends, we anticipate a new type of development as perhaps the predominant movement away from participation in formal instructional higher education in the years immediately following high school toward a more free-floating pattern of participation . . . encouraged by employer selection policies; by the development of open universities, external degree systems, and other innovations designed to stimulate a more flexible pattern of higher education experience.*[35]

Change can be an existential emetic among traditional academicians and will sometimes produce bitter criticism from those who have moved from the theoretical to the practical, particularly when they intend to make a profit at it. University of Phoenix addressed the thorny issue of the union of work and academe.

> *Besides striving to attain such a difficult goal as uniting the corporate and academic worlds, University of Phoenix's survival depends on sound management, fiscal responsibility, and being fully accountable for academic quality to the higher education community and its students. There is little doubt that the University will be closely scrutinized from all sides and cannot afford anything less than a candid relationship with all persons in contact with or affected by its existence.*[36]

Our educational delivery system was managed as a distributed enterprise with degree programs accessible without regard to geography. This system was not appropriate for education provided solely in one place, but was elemental when offered at a variety of locations. The reliance on modern management techniques was essential.

> *The mechanism chosen to realize the union of the corporate and the academic was to establish the University as a for-profit corporation. This provided the mind-set and the motivation needed to apply to the management of an institution of higher education concepts and procedures, compatible with educational principles, which have proven effective in managing private corporations producing services for individual consumers.*[37]

Use of contemporary management techniques and nomenclature in the academic world added fuel to the critics' fire. Virtually all colleges and universities manage themselves at their own pace because they rarely respond to external demands; witness the Arizona state university system's then failure to meet the needs of Arizona working adults and their employers.

The University of Phoenix, because it relied solely on its financial performance—and the performance of IPD—made executive decisions or it would be grounded on financial shoals from which it would never free itself. We couldn't go to a state legislature for an appropriation or a foundation for a grant. The integration of modern management principles and practices into the academic world demystified analogous practices at traditional institutions.

The defining difference in decision making at the University of Phoenix and traditional colleges and universities is that major decision making at traditional institutions literally consumes months and sometimes years. Many times, major academic decisions are never made at all.

CHAPTER

6

Teaching/Learning Model

The founding University of Phoenix teaching/learning model constituted a unified method of educating working adults qualified by explicit admissions standards. If any element is modified, deemphasized, or eliminated—like the provision of courses with an applied rather than theoretical content to young adults with little or no real-world experience—its educational efficacy and integrity is vitiated.

Working Adult Students

The University of Phoenix teaching/learning model differed from that observed at traditional colleges and universities because of the recognition and acceptance of the distinctions between the older adult employed full time with real-world experience, and the traditional-aged student who attends school full time with little or no real-world experience.

The Carnegie Unit teaching/learning paradigm may serve students deemed to know virtually nothing about the subject matter, but can have little or no application for older students accustomed to being active participants in, and responsible for their work and family lives.

Active Versus Passive Learning

Adults who worked a full day prior to attending evening classes—unless they are active participants—are likely to remain unengaged in the learning process. This is particularly true when the curriculum has a theoretical rather than an applied learning construct with an instructor academically qualified but not with actual experience related to subject matter application.

Traditional-aged students are typically passive learners contributing little or nothing in the classroom because of their limited knowledge and experience. Working adults commonly possess an experience base they exercise regularly in their professional and personal lives that they find both necessary and important to use as adult learners.

The founding University of Phoenix teaching/learning model permitted working adults to earn degrees while they continue to meet their full-time personal and professional responsibilities. The failure of traditional institutions to acknowledge the importance of personal and professional responsibilities of the adult learner constitutes a barrier to access. In recognition of the maturity and real-life responsibilities of adult learners, they attend class once a week for four hours and met weekly outside of class with a three-to-five-person study group.

Once a week class attendance and the independent study group requirement violates the Carnegie Unit seat-time learning equation, but the comparison is apples to oranges. University of Phoenix students, because of the design and delivery of the curriculum and the training of the instructor, were required to be active rather than passive participants in the learning process.

The Carnegie Unit learning equation turns on students being passive recipients of learning because they possess limited knowledge and experience to add constructively to material commonly presented in a lecture format. Design and delivery of University of Phoenix curriculum required adult students to assist in the presentation and discussion of curricular content individually and through study group membership. Instructors ensure adult student participation by evaluation of student participation levels individually and as study group members.

Students in classes structured on the Carnegie Unit are commonly judged to be learning by occupying a seat, but each University of Phoenix student was required to manifest evidence of learning and application of the knowledge and skills in the classroom through written work product and proactive classroom and study group participation.

Unlike many students at traditional colleges and universities, there were no anonymous learners at the University of Phoenix.

Practitioner Faculty

Traditional faculties authored courses accessible on campus primarily at times convenient to its faculty members and the institutions that employed them. University of Phoenix courses were provided at a wide variety of locations—in different cities, states, and time zones and eventually on the Internet—and taught by part-time faculty who worked full time in professions related to the subject areas in which they offered instruction. To establish and maintain quality, curriculum was developed as a corporate function.

Quality delivery of the curriculum was ensured through the requirements that all faculty members be trained in the teaching/learning model, that adult students formally evaluate all aspects of the learning experience, and the faculty and the institution assess student performance.

Passive learners at traditional institutions seldom have the opportunity to develop the skills that will allow them to succeed in the workplace, particularly the abilities to work in groups and solve problems cooperatively.

Applied Versus Theoretical Learning

Courses focused on theory in a lecture format do not ordinarily teach cooperative learning skills because they have little or no value in theoretical application. When the focus of the curriculum is the application of learning, a necessary and vital component of the learning process is the development of the affective and cognitive skills required for successful job performance.

The operative learning mechanism to achieve this objective is found in the requirement that students become members of a three-to-five-person study group for each course in which they are enrolled. Study groups were required to meet weekly outside class and were responsible for cooperative presentations of discrete elements of the subject matter for delivery in the classroom. Study group membership and participation instill and improve the skills of cooperative problem solving, an elemental part of a successful work life.

Acknowledgement of Experience

Working adult students who have assumed the responsibilities of self-supporting adulthood by working full time are familiar with cooperative decision making that incorporates their experience. They are, in effect, critical consumers of experience, and it is necessary to recognize that reality and ensure that the content of a course and the instruction reflect a healthy dose of workplace reality. Selection and training of instructors perceived as peers is essential to the credibility of the learning process.

Theoreticians in traditional classrooms may be revered by students with little or no critical experience, but can find themselves at odds with older working adult students who often possess strong opinions about the subject matter based on that experience. The recognition of this distinction in a teaching/learning model makes a critical difference in the successful provision of higher education to working adults.

Quality Control

Academic quality control in a widely distributed learning environment begins with a centrally developed curriculum that incorporates content recommendations into the curriculum by the faculty who teach in the evening what they typically practice during the day. Faculties at traditional institutions have ownership of course curricula because they are its authors, but because the curriculum at the University of Phoenix was developed by a curriculum development department, all faculty received training in both course content and its delivery in the classroom.

Faculty candidates also completed a course on the teaching/learning model and, in addition, served an internship under the direction of a faculty member. Once faculty members, they were evaluated on the conclusion of each course by every student to assess their adherence to the learning outcomes and activities specified for the course, and their success in facilitating the cooperative learning process, including study groups.

Convenience of Learning Sites

Working adults who attend traditional colleges and universities are required to dedicate limited time that could be used in the learning process to commute to a centralized campus two or three times week, find parking, sit passively in a classroom with younger, inexperienced students with whom they usually have little in common, and commute home. As the result, the learning process often brings little satisfaction, and the management of the logistics of time and place can equal the amount of time spent in the classroom.

With the establishment of learning centers in places near to where adult students live and work or through online classes, the time they would have dedicated to commuting and other logistical activities can be focused on the learning process. Degree programs commence any month of the year once a minimum number of students have enrolled in a learning group in both on-the-ground and online courses. Working adult students are not forced to accommodate themselves to an educational delivery system typically operated more for the convenience of the faculty and staff than the students.

Students as Consumers

A widely distributed learning environment requires quality-control measures that help ensure that education and services are provided at the highest levels of excellence and quality. Working adults are ordinarily critical consumers with considerable experience on which to base their assessment of the learning process and content, and it is essential to provide a formal mechanism to acknowledge their critical perceptions about the quality of all aspects of their learning experience: curriculum, instruction, learning environment, learning resources, and support services.

This critical information was obtained informally through ongoing student contact with faculty and staff, and formally through academic quality control questionnaires required to be completed at the conclusion of each course. The information produced as the result of these processes was analyzed on an ongoing basis by staff and faculty and used to improve academic programs and services.

Working adult students who have accepted responsibility for critically engaging in life through work and often family, commonly bring that attitude and experience base to the learning process. Traditional institutions, particularly ones with large numbers of younger students taking classes with limited opportunities for critical interaction, usually do not recognize the students as critical consumers of either course subject matter or of the quality of the instruction or support services.

Unified Teaching/Learning Model

When the term "unified" is used to define the University of Phoenix teaching/learning model, it means that if any element of the model is diluted, overlooked, diminished, modified, or simply missing, its educational integrity is negated. Each element of the model is integral to the successful and proper functioning of every other element. This model has virtually no application to meeting the educational needs of students without work experience and meaningful employment.

Undergraduate students are at least twenty-three, currently employed, with two years' work experience.

If students without previous college or substantive work experience are admitted, they almost always lack the experiential and intellectual basis to either understand or use learning with an applied focus. They will prove unable to contribute to or be active rather than passive learners, as required by the curriculum; are likely to fail that aspect of faculty evaluation; and are impediments to the classroom and study group learning process.

Curriculum with an applied rather than theoretical learning focus appropriate to adults who work full time.

Classes composed of adult students who meet employment, experience, and previous college learning requirements together with students who do not meet those requirements compromise the teaching/learning model because those without such qualifications cannot contribute meaningfully to the active learning process. The model is designed to integrate students' experience in learning and evaluation of course content and instruction. Without experience, students have little or no basis for substantive interaction or participation, and are likely doomed to failure.

Centrally developed curriculum based on the input of practitioner faculty and subject matter experts subject to ongoing review and revision to reflect current industry and professional practice.

If a faculty member teaching a centrally developed course based on applied professional practice does not possess the requisite real-world experience, that aspect of the learning experience for the student is deficient. The same is true for the faculty member's assessment of course content and evaluation of student performance. A similar problem arises with the requirement that students assess the value of the curriculum and instruction upon the completion of each course. They have no basis to make a useful or informed judgment.

Active rather than passive classroom environment where student participation is an elemental part of faculty evaluation.

In a classroom with students with little or no experience and no previous college work, the instructor is required to rely on a traditional lecture format. If this occurs, an applied curriculum is not suitable for passive receipt by students, and the faculty member is not trained to deliver instruction in that teaching modality. The outcomes in a scenario where students are overwhelmed by knowledge without a context and stressed by the requirement they be active participants is that they become part of dropout and student loan-default statistics.

Elements of the Unified Teaching/Learning Model

Elements essential to the optimum functioning of the University of Phoenix unified teaching/learning model include:

- Employed practitioner faculty with a minimum of five years' current professional experience in the fields related to the courses they instruct,

- Faculty completion of a comprehensive course on the teaching/learning model,
- Faculty internship in an actual course under the direction of a faculty mentor,
- Student demonstration of learning outcomes linked to independent study group participation,
- Faculty assessment of individual student achievement of learning outcomes specified for each course, and the degree to which the student actively participates in the classroom and in study groups,
- Sequential completion of one day a week, four-hour course over a period of five or six weeks, together with weekly meetings of the required study group, separate from the time spent in the classroom,
- Student assessment of each course upon completion through use of academic-quality control instruments, and
- Institutional assessment of the degree to which students achieved the learning outcomes specified for each course, independent of faculty evaluation.

CHAPTER

7

Perception Issues

There were a number of perception issues related to the University of Phoenix teaching/learning model for working adults that demanded and deserved clarification. One concern was what constitutes "quality" in higher education. This issue arose from the observation that students enrolled in nontraditional off-campus programs do not have access to the resources typically found at campus-based institutions and, therefore, quality of the education is inherently inferior.

Campus-Free

One barrier to degree program entry for working adults is a single campus operating certain months during the year primarily during the day. University of Phoenix classrooms were located in multiple geographical locations with classes offered in the evenings and on weekends.

Electronic Learning Resources

In a distributed learning environment, it is not financially feasible or necessary to construct libraries or other capital-intensive services found on traditional campuses. University of Phoenix electronic learning resources provided electronic bibliographic searches yoked to public libraries, including those at public higher education institutions, and were supplemented by electronic data analysis services.

All citizens of a state have the right to use tax-supported libraries. It was a practical solution supporting the educational needs of working adult students being served at distributed physical locations. The tax-supported postsecondary system turned up its nose, but it couldn't turn away taxpayers who underwrote the cost of its libraries.

Business Office/Student Services

We collected tuition and delivered textbooks and other course material in the first class of each course, so we didn't need a retail bookstore or business office. Our students worked full time, so we didn't need a student union, recreational facilities, or dormitories.

There were no intercollegiate sports teams or pep leaders either.

Legitimacy of For-Profit Education

Another concern is the legitimacy of higher education provided for private profit, given the hostility of higher education traditionalists toward those who provide education at a profit. Existing entirely on the largesse of a capitalist economy, higher education, after defense and health care, is the next biggest domestic expenditure of American tax dollars. Any sanctimony from traditional academics about how they earn their living versus those who pay their salaries is patently hypocritical.

At the time University of Phoenix was established, the Arizona state university system failed even to acknowledge publicly the pressing educational needs of its working adult citizens in any meaningful manner. Arizona State University opened a satellite campus to serve the north side of Phoenix a decade after University of Phoenix was accredited.

Founders of the University of Phoenix put their personal financial worth at risk in the belief that working adults needed an institution that fully acknowledged their place in society. The University of Phoenix was held accountable by its working adult students and their employers for the quality of its educational products and services, because it was charging for what public higher education institutions were giving away for free.

The result of these pioneering efforts is that the practice of traditional higher education has changed, primarily by adopting nontraditional nomenclature but rarely its academic or operational architecture. Without University of Phoenix, precious little change would have been realized. One of the reasons University of Phoenix is one of the largest private universities in the world is because the traditional higher education system still refuses, with important exceptions, to recognize the distinct status and education needs of adult learners through an educational delivery system designed specifically for their use.

Profit Motive and Educational Quality

North Central evaluators carefully examined University of Phoenix academic policies to determine whether they were actually being implemented.

Did the profit motive ever compromise its adherence to academic policies and practices?

Evaluation team after evaluation team determined that the University of Phoenix did not compromise its stated academic standards. Then, opposition to the University of Phoenix was predicated on either a prejudiced understanding of its actual academic operations or, more likely, fabricated concerns that could have been addressed if critics availed themselves of the opportunity to examine how we operated in the same objective manner as North Central evaluators.

Time to Degree

There are a number of either misinterpreted or misrepresented aspects of the teaching/learning model that made their way into the print and broadcast media.

One falsehood was that a working adult could earn a degree in a fraction of the time it would take at a traditional college or university.

At the time it was accredited, the University of Phoenix required 120 units for a bachelor's degree and 30 units for a master's degree, mirroring unit requirements at traditional colleges and universities. Students were obligated to have completed their general education requirements prior to admittance—or if requiring some, to take courses elsewhere. Many critics ignored or just refused to understand the academic structure of the University of Phoenix.

When characterizing academic programs as demanding substantially less time than traditional institutions, critics refused to acknowledge that virtually all its students had completed the first two years of college—approximately 60 credits—including those earned in the satisfaction of general education requirements. By having done so, they were responsible for earning additional credits—including those in the core curriculum—sufficient to achieve the 120-unit requirement.

It might appear to the uninformed and eagerly confused that a working adult could earn a four-year degree in two years. The reality was that students completed their third and fourth years at University of Phoenix, akin to someone who graduated from a two-year community college and transferred to a four-year institution.

In recognition that adults who work full time are materially different from younger students who attend school full time, to properly balance education and work, University of Phoenix students were required to take one course at a time, five weeks for the bachelor's program and six weeks for the master's program. Students were permitted one excused absence and were required to complete the coursework for the missed class.

The process of completing courses sequentially permitted students to concentrate on one area of study while appropriately balancing workplace and personal responsibilities.

Changing demands of work and family sometimes forced students to "stop-out" from sequential completion of coursework. Include vacations and holidays, and even highly motivated students were only able to complete between seven and nine courses a year in undergraduate programs and fewer in graduate programs.

Proceeding in this manner, students would typically earn between twenty-one and twenty-eight credits over twelve months. This is far less than the twenty-four to thirty credits that could be earned over two semesters—about seven and a half months—at traditional colleges and universities. Someone entering with two years of college would require at least another two years at University of Phoenix to earn a bachelor's degree. Master's students could complete in about a year and a half.

Violation of the Carnegie Unit

Another criticism was that a degree with limited classroom attendance—in violation of the Carnegie Unit seat-time/learning algorithm—is not academically legitimate. Younger students attending class three times a week for one hour passively listening to lectures qualifies as learning according to the teaching/learning model based on the Carnegie Unit teaching/learning paradigm; whether the seat time or study time outside of class is the predictor of learning is rarely determined.

At the University of Phoenix, where twelve to eighteen people were required to actively demonstrate engagement through presentation of course material, students had to participate actively in each class session. There were no anonymous learners because active participation was an elemental component of faculty evaluation of student performance. Every student had to complete written course assignments prior to each class and participate in a weekly study group meeting.

Since every student was required to participate actively, any failure of preparation was immediately evident. Students were also members of study groups that were included in the evaluation of their performance, and made them subject to substantial peer pressure if they failed to participate in collective assignments. Students were evaluated on achievement of learning outcomes specified for each course, including written assignments and tests, and oral presentations.

Faculty and Curriculum

Another criticism was inherent lack of curriculum quality because faculty teaching the courses did not author the curriculum. At traditional colleges and universities, each course is associated with a full-time, usually tenured, faculty member whose professional and intellectual life is dedicated to the subject matter through sustained scholarship.

Today, a high percentage of courses are taught by part-time, adjunct, non-tenure-track faculty, but the image of the dedicated, selfless scholar teaching at one institution remains extant.

An institution with a distributed learning environment, to achieve its mission of providing education with an applied, rather than a theoretical focus to full-time working adults, included current workplace, industry, and professional practices in course content. In support of the integrity and leading-edge quality of curriculum content, faculty were required to possess advanced academic degrees and five years of current practical experience substantively related to the subject matter.

University of Phoenix students were required to possess workplace experience and work full time, so courses delivered in a passive lecture format by a theoretician would possess little currency. The University of Phoenix learning environment was strengthened by a teaching/learning model that required all students to participate actively in class by being responsible, through their study groups, for helping deliver course content that incorporated experience into the delivery.

Quality Control

The binding element in the curriculum development process was the requirement that the instructor and the students be responsible for evaluating all aspects of each course upon its conclusion through completion of Academic Quality Control System questionnaires that rated not only curriculum content, relevancy, and usefulness in the workplace, but also the quality of instruction and support services like electronic learning resources and data analysis services.

Instructors and working adult students from a wide variety of companies and professions with real-world experience critically weighed in on the value and content of each course and made recommendations that were provided to curriculum developers.

Developers—together with a panel of subject-matter-qualified faculty—modified and improved the curriculum so that content remained cutting edge and relevant to workplace application. Comprehensiveness and depth of evaluation and course improvement cannot be equated to a single faculty member teaching the same primarily theoretical course year after year.

College Level Learning Through Experience

Of all the elements of the educational model for working adults that were consistently misunderstood and misrepresented was the educational soundness and validity of awarding credit that could be applied to the satisfaction of some bachelor's degree requirements through college-level learning gained through experience.

Current policy at the University of Phoenix for college credit through experience no longer specifies that credit

> *awarded through such an evaluation process evidences equivalent and discrete "college-level learning." Current policy categorically states credit will be awarded for "experience."*

Arizona state universities at the time, like the University of Phoenix, had evaluation processes established for the recognition of principal forms of learning outside college classrooms that could be applied toward the satisfaction of degree requirements:

- Courses offered by the armed services,
- Certificated learning provided by recognized non-collegiate educational entities,
- Subject matter challenge (CLEP) tests, and
- College-level learning credits awarded through the observance of the practices recommended by the then Council for the Advancement of Experiential Learning (CAEL).

A driving force behind criticism of this practice arose from University of Phoenix's profit-making status. Most critics also falsely perceived such an educational process was used with traditional-aged students with no real-world experience to evaluate. Since the University of Phoenix is only concerned about making money, academic rules and practices were allegedly bent willy-nilly to maximize profits.

In addition to the darkened status as a tax-paying higher education entity, California's diploma mills profiled in the *60 Minutes* expose issuing degrees solely for "life experience" added credibility to the denunciation of the practice.

At that time, three hundred traditional accredited higher education institutions across the nation then observed the CAEL guidelines (including the Arizona state university system), so usually one accreditation evaluator was familiar with the practice and could quickly determine whether the University of Phoenix observed recognized national standards in its own academic practices.

> *The main guideline used in assessing prior learning is the CAEL guide, Evaluation of Educational Programs in Non-Collegiate Organizations. This is supplemented by training publications and college catalogues. Outside consultants are frequently used to evaluate professional training. Administration of Justice instructors, bank program administrators, and language experts have been found by both education and experience to perform this critical function. While it is recognized that crediting college level learning is a subjective exercise, the process is solid because it is conducted according to set standards and procedures.*[38]

The recognition that documented college-level learning occurs outside a college classroom was a vital component of the University of Phoenix founding adult teaching/learning model. The assessment process compelled the working adult student to view life experience as an ongoing learning process that, when coupled with nationally recognized assessment standards and practices, was worthy of credit that could be used to the satisfaction of some degree requirements. This process has virtually no applicability to the traditional-aged student whose life experience was primarily as a student.

The University of Phoenix observed the following practices in the assessment of experience for college-level learning:

- Learning mastery must be independently verifiable—a student should be able to demonstrate the learning to an expert in the field.
- Learning should be equivalent to college-level work in quality.
- Learning should be based on knowledge of specific subject matter.
- Learning should have general applicability outside the specific situation in which it was acquired.
- There must be documentation showing the individual was present for learning to occur and a written narrative qualified for a college-level learning. Given college learning represents established norm, it must be used as the standard to compare learning gained through experience.[39]

Adult students who sought to have discrete experiences assessed to determine whether there was evidence of specific college-level learning were required to complete a Prior Learning Portfolio. The portfolio was evaluated by Prior Learning Assessment Counselors and assigned to specific subject area faculty members for evaluation. Faculty members were selected by academic discipline and professional competence to assess documented learning in their area of expertise.

During the year prior to University of Phoenix's evaluation for accreditation, we awarded a mean of

10.6 credits (8 percent) for college-level learning gained through experience that could be applied toward the 120 credits needed for graduation. Average age of the typical University of Phoenix undergraduate student was thirty-eight, with an average of nine years of work experience. This typically meant most had a meaningful number of college-level learning experiences. No letter or numerical grade was assigned.

Arizona state university system detractors sought to make the public believe degrees were awarded solely for "life experiences."

Today, based on the University of Phoenix definition of the evaluation process as being based on "experience" rather than "college level learning gained through experience," the early criticism perhaps appears not far off the mark. This was an issue identified by the North Central evaluation team in 2012 that contributed to the recommendation for accreditation probation.

CHAPTER

8

Accreditation—Arizona Regents' Attack

Clear the smoke and dust from the Arizona state higher education system and University of Phoenix melee, and it proves vexing why the state system—by attacking the University of Phoenix—attacked taxpaying Arizona working adult citizens' right to select education that met their personal and professional needs.

North Central Accreditation

North Central accreditation is a multilayered evaluation and review process conducted by independent senior academics and administrators drawn from over one thousand mostly traditional public and private colleges and universities in its nineteen state region. If an institution operates in different accrediting regions, representatives from those regions are also included as members of evaluation teams. No one from North Central participating in the evaluation of an institution for accreditation can work at another institution in the same state or have any other connection.

This conflict of interest policy helps ensure evaluations are conducted in an unbiased, objective manner. The Arizona state university system allegation that the University of Phoenix bought—de facto—its candidacy evidenced a dreary understanding of accreditation and self-important lack of respect for the academic professionals who voluntarily participate in it.

There are so many individuals from different colleges and universities conducting North Central evaluations and reviews, wholly independent of other evaluations and reviews, that it is virtually impossible to "buy" or materially influence decision making of the scores of people exercising such self-determining roles. The University of Phoenix was evaluated, like every other candidate, according to standard policies and procedures.

- The application constituted prima facie evidence that we met the then thirteen North Central General Institutional Requirements.
- An institutional self-study comprehensively described academic and financial operations, and assessed the degree to which our academic goals and objectives were achieved. A core element is the involvement of the board of directors, administrative staff, faculty, and students in the process. Upon approval of the self-study by North Central executive staff, it is provided to an on-site evaluation team.

- Team members are chosen from a roster of trained evaluators from different institutions outside the state of the college or university being considered.
- The team conducts an on-site evaluation to determine the extent to which the mission, goals, and objectives were achieved evidenced through an assessment of documentation—including student work products—and private meetings with the board of directors, staff, faculty, and students. Every aspect of our academic operation was verified including adherence to published academic policies, qualifications of faculty, content and quality of curriculum, evaluation of student performance, financial policies and practices, learning resources, and independence of the board. The team seeks to identify disparities between what the institution professes to be doing and what it is actually doing. The conclusion of the visit is a team meeting with the administration to report on strengths and weaknesses and the recommendation it will make to the commission.
- The team chair authors a report provided to a review committee composed of senior academics and administrators from colleges and universities outside the state of the institution being evaluated. The review committee is provided the self-study, report of the visiting team, and any response to the team report by the institution. We could attend the review committee to answer questions and provide additional information to assist them in determining whether to approve or reject the recommendation of the on-site evaluation team, or make their own recommendation.

- The review committee findings and recommendations are provided to the North Central Commission on Institutions of Higher Education—now Higher Learning Commission—along with the self-study, the report of the on-site evaluation team, the report of the review committee and its recommendations, and the institutional response.
- If an appeal is made of the site team's or review committee's recommendations, the evaluation corpus goes from the commission to the executive board.

Given the comprehensive, multilevel evaluation structure to help ensure unbiased, objective evaluation by individuals from a variety of institutions outside the state of the institution being evaluated, the assertion that the University of Phoenix, or any other candidate institution, could "purchase" or have material political influence on a North Central accreditation decision is wholly without merit.

Regents' Ambush

The Arizona state university system's political ambush of the University of Phoenix was orchestrated at a regents' meeting just months after its executive coordinator personally assured John Sperling that any institution seeking accreditation from North Central was welcome in Arizona. Prior to his contact with John Sperling, the executive coordinator claimed there were 300 diploma mills in Arizona.[40]

During a two-day meeting covered by the news media, the same executive coordinator laid the political foundation for legislation for the regents seizure of control over private higher education licensure in Arizona. If passed, the University of Phoenix would be denied licensure and its candidacy for accreditation revoked.

The executive coordinator symbolically trephined the regents' and state university system's florid paranoia about the postnatal presence of the University of Phoenix:

> *Number one: we want to bring back our friend the establishment of a postsecondary, ah . . . bill . . . We are literally being flooded. I have never seen a state in my life that has received as many of these things as we have in the last year. They're coming at us from all sides and they're beginning to affect the ability of the universities and the community colleges to provide quality education to the citizens of the state.*[41]

The claim that diploma mills were *beginning to affect the ability of the universities and community colleges to provide quality education* when Arizona's tax-supported higher education institutions enrolled 98.3 percent of all postsecondary students was specious, but resonated stoutly with many members of the legislature, a public in awe of their state university system, and a childishly impressionable news media.

> *Ah, one that came down the pike, which I will mention a bit more to the president's agenda, recently, ah . . . . strikes at the very heart, in my opinion, of our accreditation system. It would appear that the North Central Association has lowered their accreditation requirements to the extent of actually recommending accreditation for people who have no campus, who have no classrooms, who have no libraries, who use evaluation of life services . . . cranked into your BA, and in some cases you can bypass your BA altogether*

> *and go straight into a masters or doctoral program.*[42]

Not one diploma mill had been identified, but the artfully credulous—particularly some members of the news media—were convinced that Arizona public higher education was in mortal peril. The following day, the executive coordinator continued to construct his Grand Canyon diploma mill of cards.

> *Mr. President, I referred to this briefly yesterday when we were talking about legislation. As I said at the time, we are literally being flooded in this state with every conceivable type of educational institution, if you want to call them that, imaginable. Now to check this floodgate, and it is a floodgate because most other states have already put in legislation, say in Texas, for example which they did just last year, they begin to look for a new home and practically everybody who was operating in Texas has now moved to Phoenix. Mr. President, although University of Phoenix is used as an example, I don't want you to think that we are zeroing in on them particularly. There are as many others that are just as bad and some a lot, lot worse.*[43]

The executive coordinator publicly claimed that *every conceivable type* of diploma mill was inundating Arizona, but the sole institution identified during his pontificating on the waterless flood of trick degrees was the University of Phoenix.

> *The Arizona Board of Regents expressed concern over the possible accreditation of University of Phoenix . . . . and members were told that out-of-state academic institutions which are not accredited likely*

> *will flood the state unless legislation to prohibit their operation is passed next year.*[44]

Readily available was the corporate status of the University of Phoenix, identities of the well-known public members of its board, and its acceptance as a candidate for accreditation from the recognized higher education body that accredited all Arizona educational institutions.

Reporters from the *Arizona Republic* and its afternoon sister paper, the *Phoenix Gazette,* and from other Arizona news media, never verified even one of the regents' claims.

> *ASU officials and the Arizona Board of Regents are worried that a college in Phoenix will become accredited, because no one seems to know where the college is or what it offers.*[45]

Befuddled, bothered, and bewildered were the regents and officials of Arizona State University. They knew North Central had accepted the University of Phoenix for candidacy, and believed it somehow did so even through no one at Arizona State could physically locate the University of Phoenix, nor find out information about its principals or academic programs.

This threadbare drivel was the political lingua franca that militated Arizona public and legislative support for the regents' seizure of licensure over private higher education.

> *"The legislature in the past has considered some steps against diploma mills which give out diplomas for a fee," Crowder said. "Although the legislature has been down on diploma mills, I think University of Phoenix is much more of a threat than a fake diploma, and I don't know how the legislature will react, . . .* [46]

In testament to the regents' and state university system executives' lack of knowledge of accreditation—and possessing virtually no respect for it—they established in the minds of the public and the legislature the high desert phantasm that the University of Phoenix *was much more of a threat than a fake diploma.*

> *U. Of PHX?: REGENTS CALL IT 'DIPLOMA MILL.' ASU ACCEPTS TRANSFER CREDITS.*
> *The Arizona Board of Regents is up in arms because the organization that accredits Arizona universities is considering accreditation of a school they term a "diploma mill." Sounds like a bargain, doesn't it? ASU President John Schwada said, "These places are springing up all over. It's stunning to me that they are in existence."*[47]

Repeated efforts to get the regents and the state universities to justify their allegations or issue retractions were uniformly ignored.

> *REGENTS OUT TO CRUSH "DIPLOMA MILLS."*
> *The influx of so-called "diploma mills" will prompt the state universities this year to make their programs accessible throughout the state, the outgoing president of the Arizona Regents predicts. Regent Rudy Campbell of Tempe said Arizona is easy prey to schools that offer substandard education while granting traditional degrees. Texas recently tightened its licensing of schools, which may lead many such institutions to move to Arizona. But Campbell said "I think there might be a good chance that the Arizona Legislature will take steps to head off the problem," which he views as a major issue facing the universities in 1978.*[48]

It remains ludicrous to imagine how a private institution with eight working adult students, with known and respected Arizonans on its board, and accepted for accreditation candidacy by the sole legitimizing accrediting agency for higher education in Arizona, became the *major issue facing the Arizona state universities.* The representation was infantile, but the University of Phoenix was in lethal political straits.

It is exceedingly difficult to dispel irrational claims by any powers-that-be, particularly a state university system believed to possess minds trained in determining objective fact and a moral compass to guide it.

> *DEGREE SITUATION EXAMINED.*
> *REGULATORY NEED UNDERLINED*
> *(The) executive coordinator for the Arizona Board of Regents said today that the proposed legislation to license and regulate postsecondary educational institutions is not aimed at any one organization. Woodall, who introduced the problem of private, degree-granting colleges and universities at the November Regents' meeting, denies his comments were directed against University of Phoenix. Woodall said that 43 states have such licensing procedures and that Arizona has become a prime location for many to move into because there is no regulation. The flap arose over the candidacy status of University of Phoenix which was used as an example during discussions of "diploma mills" in November.*[49]

Murphy's Law of Political Theater

My immutable law of political theater is to accept, at face value, whatever the opposition says or claims about you no matter how personally affronting, financially devastating, politically effective, or palpably dimwitted.

I visited the office of the Arizona attorney general and asked for the locations of the 300 Arizona diploma mills alleged by the executive coordinator of the regents; neither the criminal nor civil fraud units identified one. I posed the same question to the board of education, the vocational education board, and the commission on postsecondary education. Individually and collectively, none knew of any diploma mill in Arizona.

About the time the University of Phoenix opened its doors, a man run out of another state for operating an actual diploma mill established a mail drop "university" in Tempe, home to Arizona State University. Exposed in the media, he eventually got out of Dodge.

A criminal fraud investigator in the attorney general's office contacted the office of the Texas attorney general about its diploma mill problem. Texas had no problem for a year and no one knew of any diploma mill that migrated to Arizona.

Equipped with my thorough documentation of Arizona's protracted diploma mill draught, John Sperling requested to make a presentation before the regents. John was not allowed to speak during the legislative agenda where the regents conducted the diploma mill media ambush, but was shoe-horned into the public comment item at the tail end of the meeting after the media had departed.

Hostility was conspicuous when John rose to speak. Narrowed eyes and tight-lipped scowls skewed the expressions of the regents, and state university staff sardined into the room raised their eyebrows and sniffed grimly.

Instantly upon the conclusion of John's brief presentation, the chair glanced cursorily at the mum regents and the meeting was adjourned without comment.

The battleground had just become the Arizona legislature.

CHAPTER

9

"Education is Not as Sudden as a Massacre."[50]

What would you have done if you were an Arizona state university system executive who believed the University of Phoenix was *worse than a diploma mill,* and was given the opportunity to freely evaluate its academic operations?

At the urging of our North Central consultants, we invited state university representatives to visit.

In the parking lot prior to entering our tiny offices in downtown Phoenix, three state university executives and a member of the regents' staff reportedly agreed among themselves not to examine any documentation or ask any questions. During their stilted two-hour visit, their behavior affirmed the reported agreement made in the parking lot; all exhibited an absolute disengagement with the documentation and a self-congratulatory conspiracy of silence.

As if attacked by the British at what proved to be the start of the American Revolution, the Arizona state university system responded to University of Phoenix candidacy for accreditation by first blowing out the flame, then waving a darkened lantern from their ivory tower to warn everyone the diploma mills were coming.

Instead of objectively determining the precise nature of our nontraditional educational model for working adults, critics leveraged their status at a tax-supported higher education system to promote a distorted and factually deficient description of our academic operations. They got away with it for years, but it ultimately proved so unimaginative, that by adhering to our educational principles and practices, we were able to overcome virtually all of its intended consequences.

Arizona state university system academics critical of the University of Phoenix were steeped in traditional higher education. It solely constituted quality learning. They confined themselves to a single campus where faculty and staff are dedicated to the institution and the provision of education in a proven, classical manner; a rarified world, where in recognition of its lofty goals—in the main—it operates only a limited number of months of the year, usually during the day.

Students are primarily young and impressionable, attend full time, and are instructed by academic professionals who dedicate themselves to the institution and strengthening of subject matter expertise through ongoing scholarship. It's a place where the crass demands of capitalism are kept morally at bay, yet one that receives billions of tax dollars from a citizenry who values and honors its quintessential place in the American Dream.

From this tax-supported redoubt, the Arizona state university system dry-gulched the University of Phoenix after being provoked by a private institution with a student body of eight working adults taking the sole path to higher education legitimacy: regional accreditation.

Diploma Mill Bill

We commenced political activity in the Arizona House of Representatives because the chair of the House Education Committee, Coolidge Arizona dairyman Jim Cooper, was the lead author of the regents' diploma mill legislation.

There existed a high level of confusion about accreditation besieged with the clammy belief that the state was flooded with diploma mills. We explained the University of Phoenix had chosen the only option available to establish academic legitimacy: accreditation from the same body that accredited all Arizona educational institutions. Most legislators agreed accreditation was—whatever it was—a good thing. They took the word of the state university system because they believed it defined higher education quality.

"Your fight is not with the legislature; it's with the state university system. Convince them you're legitimate and you'll have no problem with us."

Legislators viewed higher education primarily through capital-intensive expenditures at a physical campus. We explained how Arizona working adults were prevented from completing degrees by attending classes at often-great distances from where they lived and worked. We spoke of the need of employers for degree programs that were accessible to their employees, and recognized and accommodated their status as full-time working adults.

The state university system made no differentiation between the younger and older student, whereas the University of Phoenix observed that distinction through the provision of courses with an applied rather than a theoretical focus, instructors with current professional experience related to the courses they instructed, and classrooms near to where the students lived and worked.

Run that by me again . . . slowly.

An educational approach is tenuous with any public official, but we had no choice. We also zeroed in on an innate sentiment that private education should not be under the control of a public system. If the regents' bill passed, they would control all private higher education, including sectarian schools. If the regents could decide which private institutions would and would not be allowed to operate, the Arizona public higher education monopoly would be complete.

Meeting With the Chairman

Chairman Cooper commenced his individual meeting with us by expressing his outrage that three hundred diploma mills were operating in Arizona. We advised him that no law enforcement, public higher education regulatory or planning agency identified even one.

Cooper thundered:

"I don't care if there aren't any diploma mills, if the regents say there are, then as far as this committee is concerned, there are!"

John Sperling:

"What would happen to a dairyman if someone falsely said that his milk cows had Bang's disease?"

Cooper:

"No one would buy my milk, and if I didn't disprove the false charge right away, I could lose my livelihood."

Sperling allowed that the University of Phoenix was in a similar situation because it had been falsely labeled a diploma mill that would be forced from existence if the regents' bill passed.

Cooper literally sat back in his seat for a few very thoughtful moments.

It proved to be the beginning of a slowly developing, but an eventually long and mutually respectful relationship.

Diploma Mill Bill Hearing

The dark wood veneer-paneled legislative hearing room in the Arizona state capitol where the evening debate on the Arizona regents' diploma mill bill was held was elbow to elbow with lathered-up regents' and state university employees eager to witness their first, and probably only, higher education *auto-da-fe*.

The regents gripped one University of Phoenix appendage, and the University of Arizona, Arizona State University, and Northern Arizona University were angled to rip off the others.

Oddly, a large television on a portable stand faced House Education Committee members seated behind a massive U-shaped table on a dais. We developed rapport among a few members. We didn't have the votes to stop the bill, but had established the need for discussion.

Chairman Cooper acknowledged a state university system representative who rose to announce gravely that the regents' sole testimony in support of their bill would be the television screening of a recent CBS *60 Minutes* expose on State of California licensed diploma mills.

Our embryonic credibility proved friable as committee members absorbed the highly charged mass market hit piece. Jaws set and eyes flashed. Smirks on the faces of the state university system employees trumpeted that the *60 Minutes* surrogate for testimony was a political home run. The self-righteousness was suffocating.

The University of Phoenix was circling the inside of the state university system's toilet bowl when Chairman Cooper recognized committee member, James Sossaman, a cattleman from Prescott, Arizona. Sossaman was spitting mad. He never acknowledged our perspective on the regents' bill and I thought he was going to pile on.

Stunningly, Sossaman exploded in outrage about the state university system's repellant scheme of substituting—as its sole testimony—a highly prejudicial, hot-button mass media hit piece on an actual diploma mill problem in another state to importune the committee to vote for legislation that would place private higher education under control of the regents. He didn't give a damn about the University of Phoenix, but was affronted by a soap-opera tactic that exploited emotion over an objective hearing on a fundamental policy issue.

When it was our turn to testify, the atmosphere in the hearing room was so leaden that John Sperling's presentation went utterly unheard by committee members glancing longingly and repeatedly at the exits behind the dais.

The regents' diploma mill bill passed unanimously and the committee members bolted.

The University of Phoenix was a blink shy of a death rattle.

We didn't realize it until later, but for powerful players in both political parties, Representative Sossaman had gutted the state university system's life and death grip on the public/private licensure issue. Most state university system employees were ignorant of his principled criticism of their reprehensible political theater.

No one posed the question: since California licensed diploma mills, why didn't the University of Phoenix forget accreditation and move there?

We needed to establish a broader community of interest in legislation that would empower the regents to control the licensure of private colleges and universities. In response, I—together with Paul Daly, the president of Embry-Riddle Aeronautical University in Prescott—subsequently founded the Independent Colleges and Universities of Arizona (ICUA).

Paul and I hosted a meeting of the handful of Arizona private higher education institutions, American Graduate School of International Management, DeVry Institute (now university), Embry-Riddle Aeronautical University in Prescott, Grand Canyon College. Embry-Riddle and Prescott Center College agreed to join, DeVry didn't join but participated, and the American Graduate School and Grand Canyon College (now University) would have nothing to do with it.

The issue of granting the regents control over private higher education—together with documentation that Arizona had not one diploma mill—gained purchase on more and more legislators.

We attracted spontaneous allies: Arizona Bankers' Association, Arizona Taxpayers' Association, and a community college lobbyist who was a Yaqui Indian. His tribe experienced unpleasant things at the hands of Arizona's tax-supported powers-that-be and he hated bullies. Dino DeConcini provided entrée to Democrats, and we employed a lobbyist for one of Arizona's largest industries.

He insisted we not acknowledge him in the halls of the legislature.

Opposition to the regents' bill began to coalesce because of the towering avarice of the state university system that annually pressed for greater and greater shares of the state budget while refusing—as we informed legislators—to meet the educational needs of Arizona working adults and their employers.

The tide shifted in the Senate Education Committee hearing when a member of the regents' staff engaged in legislative bait and switch:

> *(T)he bill has been mistakenly dubbed a diploma mill bill. Institutions which are actual diploma mills can be handled under existing statutes.*[51]

The bill squeaked past the Senate Education Committee, but died a less than ignominious death on the senate floor at the hands of the Republican majority.

The Independent Colleges and Universities of Arizona subsequently got legislation enacted to restrict licensure to academic degree-granting higher education institutions that were regionally accredited, were candidates for accreditation, or were applicants for candidacy. No entities hallucinated as diploma mills have ever established operations in Arizona.

Neither the *Arizona Republic* nor *Phoenix Gazette* gave credit to the University of Phoenix and the Independent Colleges and Universities of Arizona for its authorship and enactment.

Institutional Self-Study

Throughout the time the regents' diploma mill bill was being considered, John Sperling and I spent literally every other waking moment not lobbying for our survival, writing an institutional self-study that detailed and critically evaluated the University of Phoenix's academic, governance, and financial operations. An elemental part was an assessment of the degree to which the University of Phoenix achieved the educational goals and objectives contained in its mission and purposes statement.

> *Most of the University functions—receptionist, registrar, and curriculum developers—were housed in a large open space on the second floor. This is where John Murphy and I fought the crucial battle of accreditation with our minds and our pens. An institution prepares for an accreditation visit by writing a self-study that, for us, was a carefully reasoned argument as to why UOP should be granted accreditation. We wrote two mock self-studies and countless drafts of the self-study itself. We sat at a long table with yellow pads scribbling away with pencils and editing with scissors and paste sticks. When we had a "final" yellow-paper draft, we had it typed. Then, being the good old days before word processing, we further edited by literally cutting and pasting. Working in this fashion, we had constant contact with all of the staff and the faculty and students who dropped in. It is not an exaggeration to say that every member of the University was involved in the process and all had immediate input. They all understood that the future of the University depended on the quality and persuasiveness of what we were writing.*[52]

We retained two accreditation consultants, both from the team that conducted the evaluation for candidacy: Drs. Donald Roush and Wade Ellis.

An institutional self-study is an almanac used by on-site evaluators to comprehensively examine every aspect of an institution under consideration for accreditation or reaffirmation of accreditation. Nothing or no one is off the record.

We documented the degree to which the University of Phoenix was achieving its educational goals and objectives. This formidable task was accomplished—in addition to the quality of the curriculum, faculty, and student work products—through creation of the Academic Quality Management System. In its infancy, what was initially called the Academic Accounting System consisted of questionnaires students and faculty completed at the conclusion of each course.

Questions ranged from the mundane—convenience of class sites, parking, restrooms, furniture and fixtures—to a detailed rating of all aspects of the academic experience: curriculum, administrative support, faculty performance, value of the program, value of learning activities, effectiveness and value of study groups, value of fellow students as learning resources, and quality and value of academic information services.

> *The data . . . indicate that there has been . . . improvement in Administrative Services but that much remains to be done. Facilities are uniformly satisfactory but the Academic Information Services needs improvement, and this has been given high priority. Instruction remains a bright spot in the program and the ratings vary little throughout the length of the*

program. The portfolio process [mechanism for the assessment of college level learning gained through experience] received mediocre ratings which arises from two major problems: the first is that the process is anxiety laden; second, and more important, the process is not yet as effective and efficient as it should be. The University has established a task force to study the portfolio process. . . . Four uniformly high ratings, which do much to validate the University's pedagogical philosophy, are those for effectiveness of Small Groups, the value of fellow students as a learning resource, the Project/Thesis, and the academic/work interface. The final ratings in the Overall Quality of the program, the Value to the Student, Convenience of Time and Place, and Satisfaction with Regard to Cost remain very high and it is doubtful that improving program components will lead to a significant improvement in these ratings.[53]

The self-study also identifies external problems affecting the achievement of an institution's mission. External political problems vastly overawed internal problems. This was a rare circumstance for a fledgling nontraditional higher education institution endeavoring to implement controversial educational innovations; that was difficult enough. We categorized this aspect of our academic universe as "External Problems and Possibilities."

Given the pitched battle in the legislature and toxic public effects of the brutal political ambush by the Arizona state university system, our categorization was more appropriate to a Saguaro appreciation society.

CHAPTER

10

Evaluation for Accreditation

The regulatory structure of higher education favors traditional nonprofit public and private colleges and universities, and though the University of Phoenix was granted candidacy for accreditation, we were treated differently because of our tax status. Candidacy of nonprofit and public higher education institutions brings eligibility for federal Title IV student loans. For-profit institutions must achieve accreditation before eligibility attaches. Employer tuition assistance is ordinarily restricted to accredited but not candidate institutions.

The University of Phoenix maintained its Arizona license and satisfied the threshold North Central General Institutional Requirement. Given our poisoned public image, however, we were compelled to request an evaluation for accreditation the second year of candidacy before the students from the St. Mary's consortium and our eight students graduated. Thousands of Arizona working adults wanted what we offered, but not until accredited.

> *The battle for accreditation was a battle for survival. The minimum time that could lapse between the grant of candidate status and the application for accreditation was two years. Only one or perhaps two newly created institutions of higher education had ever achieved accreditation in that short time, but UOP had no choice but to make the attempt.*[54]

North Central approved the draft self-study and Thurston Manning selected three distinguished academics for the evaluation team.

> *The team was chaired by Francis Heller, the Roy Roberts Professor of Law and Political Science at the University of Kansas; the other members were Albert Sussman, Dean of the Graduate School at the University of Michigan, and Ray Heffner, Professor of English and former academic vice president at the University of Iowa.*[55]

The team reportedly received a visit at their hotel the night prior to the evaluation visit by representatives of the Arizona state university system. The team recommended continued candidacy, allegedly because of our limited track record. Continued candidacy is usually not viewed as a disability, but because of the septic political atmosphere created by the Arizona state university system, our detractors characterized anything we sought, but didn't get, as a catastrophic failure and proof of their criticisms.

We appealed recommendation of continued candidacy to the review panel that would assess the visiting team's report. The review panel would approve or disapprove the team's recommendation or issue a new recommendation. The evaluation record and team and review panel recommendations for continued candidacy were provided to the executive board of the commission. They ruled the University of Phoenix stay in candidacy. The North Central Executive Board permitted reapplication in one year rather than the customary two years.

> *Although the Executive Board probably considered that the best they could do given the political pressure from the Arizona universities, it was of no value to UOP, because UOP would no longer be in existence in another year. We knew that the members of the commission had been heavily lobbied, and we were informed that the reversal came only after threats of secession from the North Central Association by Arizona's three state universities. The Arizona Board of Regents, in what was certainly an unprecedented action by a governing board of a state university system, had joined with Arizona academics in an attempt to force the Commission to rule against University of Phoenix and deny accreditation.*[56]

The *eminence grise* behind Arizona state university system's antipathy toward the University of Phoenix would later prove to be WASC. There is little doubt that IPD's California legislative initiative played a seminal role in its subsequent collaboration with the Arizona state university system to destroy the University of Phoenix. John Sperling and I flew to Las Cruces, New Mexico to meet with Don Roush and draft a petition requesting the grant of accreditation based on the team report and the recommendation of the review committee.

The executive board ordered another fact-finding visit. An on-site team had evaluated the University of Phoenix; a review panel examined the evaluation results; the commission assessed the results of the visit and review panel findings; and the executive board examined the evaluation corpus. Now, barely two months after the on-site evaluation visit, there would be yet another visit.

The fact-finding team composed of G. Philip Johnson, Dean of Graduate Study at Oakland University, Rochester, Michigan, and Donald Robinson, Dean of the College of Education at Oklahoma State, found:

> *"(The) institution was better able to abide by Association standards than did our colleagues on the [accreditation] team."*[57]

The operative question had become whether the integrity of the North Central accreditation evaluation and decision making process with the University of Phoenix had been compromised politically by the Arizona state university system. Diehard political interference from the Arizona state university system forced North Central Commission on Institutions of Higher Education to evaluate the integrity of its own accreditation evaluation and decision making process as much as it was evaluating the University of Phoenix.

John Sperling and I drafted a petition seeking reconsideration of the executive board's decision to continue candidacy. The petition went to a committee on reconsideration: Sr. Ida Gannon, Mundeline College, Chicago, chairperson; President Tilghman Aley, Casper College; Professor Joseph Cosand, University of Michigan, Ann Arbor; Professor Robert Keller, University of Minnesota,

Minneapolis; and Vice President William Neptune, Oklahoma Baptist University.

The committee recommended the University of Phoenix be granted accreditation.

The next meeting of the executive board was not for six months when they would either grant accreditation or continue candidacy. Continued candidacy was a death sentence.

Of the thousands of places for the executive board to meet in North Central's nineteen state region, it selected Tucson, home of the University of Arizona. The state university system would continue to politicize the accreditation of the University of Phoenix from the comfort of its own backyard.

> *Not only were members of the North Central Board bombarded with stories of UOP's scandalous practices, I [Sperling] was accused of purchasing the support of Dr. John Prince, a member of the UOP Board of Directors who had just retired as Chancellor of the Maricopa County Community College System, and Doctors Ellis and Roush, our two North Central consultants.*[58]

Deferral of the accreditation decision provided the state university system a leisurely schedule of political manipulation while we were left dangling in the wind unable to recruit a single student.

There was nothing material that could be added to the evaluation corpus and no students would enroll until accreditation had been awarded. I performed continuing ad hoc consulting work for John Sperling, but left to publish and edit the *Family Journal of Mental Health* and write a novel based on a kidnapping, murder, and lynching that occurred in San Jose, California, in 1933.

James "Sunny Jim" Rolph, California's governor, promised to pardon all lynchers the night before the lynching and repeated the same thing the next morning after the hanging deaths of two across the street from the county jail witnessed by a middle class mob estimated by the press to have totaled as many as 15,000 people.

The novel went unpublished, the *Family Journal* didn't survive financially, and I rejoined John Sperling. After I resigned from the University of Phoenix, I wrote the screenplay—*Valley of the Heart's Delight (Valley of Heart's Delight was* the nickname of *Silicon Valley* when millions of fruit trees existed*)*—based on the lynching and produced an award-winning feature film of the same title.

John Sperling took a new political tack. Corporate counsel was a friend of the governor of Arizona, Bruce Babbitt, an ex officio member of the regents, and arranged a confidential luncheon.

> *The degree of confidentiality was evidenced by the fact that the luncheon was served in a private hotel suite, and the governor entered the building through the service entrance and used a service elevator. Governor Babbitt was both understanding and gracious. In his opinion, University of Phoenix was providing a useful service to the community and the attempt of the state universities to destroy it was territorialism at its most unattractive. The governor assured me that he was not, and could not be an advocate of UOP, but he was and could be an advocate of fairness and due process. He said that he would urge the members of the Board of*

Regents to cease their lobbying efforts and to "allow the process to work."[59]

The second week of December, John Sperling, Don Roush, and Wade Ellis checked into the Tucson hotel where the North Central executive board would decide whether the University of Phoenix would live or die.

The morning passed, lunch was eaten in silence, and optimism turned into apprehension. After lunch I ventured into the hallway outside the room where the Directors were meeting, and the loud and angry voices from within served only to increase our apprehensions.[60]

The meeting mercifully concluded early in the evening. The University of Phoenix had been granted accreditation with a focus visit in two years.

The Arizona state university system scathingly denigrated the accreditation because it had been granted on appeal. The following year, the regents introduced another diploma mill bill but with the help of the Independent Colleges and Universities of Arizona, and behind-the-scenes work by representatives of religious schools worried about the precedent of a public higher education board controlling private education, the bill failed.

Despite the eye-catching victory over the Arizona state university system, the University of Phoenix's fight for survival had only just begun.

CHAPTER

11

Arizona Regents' Attempts to Secede From North Central—AACRAO

The Arizona state university system failed to compromise the integrity of North Central, but remained uncompromisingly determined to destroy the University of Phoenix. The regents next sought to make Arizona part of the WASC accrediting region.

Should this transfer of regions have succeeded, all Arizona and public and private colleges and universities and K-12 schools would have to be accredited by WASC.

We had to stop the secession.

In California, IPD contracts with the University of San Francisco, followed by St. Mary's College and the University of Redlands, were not renewed. The termination of these contracts eliminated revenue and tossed IPD staff into the street.

A deadly economic problem was embraced as an opportunity. Existing IPD California offices and classroom sites were transformed into University of Phoenix campuses. It was accomplished seamlessly because California observed a reciprocity policy of recognizing all regional accreditation for licensure as an academic degree-granting institution. IPD possessed experienced employees motivated to make the University of Phoenix successful. If the California contracts had been renewed, we would not have entered the state until a much later date.

WASC had engendered the rapid-fire establishment of the University of Phoenix in California.

Seven months following the award of accreditation—in affirmation of the Arizona regents secession initiative—WASC approved the gerrymandering of North Central and WASC regions to make Arizona part of WASC. There was virtually no concern this change would have negative personal and economic consequences to University of Phoenix's working adult students, their employers, the economy, public K-12 schools, or Arizona taxpayers.

Six justifications were proffered by the Arizona regents for the "transfer" to WASC:

- Use of objective evaluation standards by the Senior Commission of the Western Association,
- Geographical reasons—distance from other states in the North Central Association and time differences,
- The large number of members in North Central versus small membership in WASC,
- Affiliation with schools in the PAC 10, which are members of WASC,
- Membership costs for postsecondary schools accredited are the same as in North Central and,

- Affiliation of Arizona with other western states.

The justifications benefit from decoding for those unfamiliar with the reliably unfathomable nature of higher education politics.

> ***Objective Evaluation Standards***
>
> All institutions, independent of mission, goals, and objectives, must meet traditional standards. Objective standards include full-time faculty, single campus, library, and observation of the Carnegie Unit seat-time/learning equation.
>
> ***Geographical Distances from Other North Central States and Time Differences***
>
> California, but not Arizona, observes daylight savings. Between April (now March) and October, the people of Arizona and California suffer the ruinous consequences of being one hour apart despite the states being contiguous.
>
> ***Large Number of Members in North Central Versus the Small Number in WASC***
>
> Control over the practice of higher education without conflict of interest rules.
>
> ***Membership in the PAC 10***
>
> This confirms the worst suspicions about the unhealthy influence of collegiate sports on higher education. Membership in a collegiate athletic conference is not among any regional association's accreditation requirements.

> ***Membership Costs the Same as North Central***
>
> This fails to account for the tax dollars that would be expended to have WASC conduct comprehensive accreditation evaluations of all Arizona educational institutions, including K-12 schools.
>
> ***Affiliation with Western States***
>
> Arizona's public higher education hobby horse riders didn't cotton to North Central tinhorns who failed to be in awe of their devil-may-care, bushwhacking, wide-open range, rope them doggies, shoot-first-and-ask-later, tumbleweed-tossed, sidewinder-infested, heaving with adventure, wild, wild, wild west.

You won't sell any of that twaddle to the Arizona air conditioning industry.

In most other states, such an ill-conceived and flaccid proposal would be dismissed as being totally off the wall, but literally anything was possible in Arizona higher education politics. We now had to expend limited resources to stop the proposed transfer of accreditation regions. Because of the impact of secession on all Arizona educational institutions, it attracted legislative interest.

We approached Arizona House of Representatives Republican majority leader, Burton Barr, and persuaded him to conduct an inquiry into the proposed "transfer." Barr was experienced in higher education politics because of his prominent role in obtaining appropriations for the Arizona state university system.

None of the reasons cited, separately, or in total, justify the transfer of accreditation. Such a move would be justified if the end result would be greatly improved educational programs. This reason has not been mentioned. Because none of the reasons cited . . . appear valid, there is an indication that other matters have influenced the proposed transfer. The accreditation of University of Phoenix by the North Central Association was met with heavy opposition from the state universities. . . . The final accreditation of University of Phoenix . . . precipitated more serious discussions about the current proposal.[61]

Contemptuously ignoring the majority leader's findings, the regents single-mindedly pursued the transfer of accrediting regions.

The regents' effort kerplopped into a discomfiting heap when the organization of Arizona K-12 school boards, apparently horrified at the specter of Californians wielding dissolute power over primary and secondary education in Arizona, belatedly skidded forward to kill the transfer.

American Association of Collegiate Registrars and Admission Officers (AACRAO)

The University of Phoenix had now defeated the Arizona state university system three times in a row:

1. Killed legislation to place private higher education under the regents;
2. Achieved accreditation despite a full-court political press; and
3. Prevented the transfer of Arizona to the WASC region.

What else could they possibly do to us?
They never failed to fail us.

To facilitate recognition of degrees and credits, the "flagship" land-grant higher education institution in each state submits degree and transfer-credit recognition policies toward all other accredited institutions in its state to the American Association of Collegiate Registrars and Admissions Officers (AACRAO) for publication in its national transfer credit guide.

The AACRAO guide issued after University of Phoenix accreditation codified that the degrees and credits of every accredited Arizona higher education institution were acceptable to the University of Arizona—the "flagship" institution—except the University of Phoenix.

Students, potential students, graduates, and employers soon reported the state universities did not recognize University of Phoenix degrees or accept transfer credits. The policy not only affected Arizona enrollment, but our students and graduates seeking admission at every accredited college or university in the national AACRAO guide.

Registrars and admissions officers use the degree and transfer credit recognition policy of the flagship institution in each state in lieu of having to conduct an independent review of every institution an applicant attended. AACRAO did not intend its guide to be used for other reasons, but many corporate human resources departments often wrongfully relied on it for purposes of recognizing degrees for employment.

The University of Arizona refused to change the policy and we challenged AACRAO. It responded that it did not establish policies, just published them. Positive policies facilitate educational commerce. Those that are negative deny a specific class of students and graduates equal standing with the students and graduates of other accredited colleges and universities.

We advised AACRAO that the publication of the policy made it liable for any harm it caused the University of Phoenix because it would have no national currency without publication. The guide was an instrument of nationwide discrimination against a class of people—University of Phoenix students and graduates—and we would commence legal action if they published the policy. AACRAO temporized and claimed publication was postponed because of unresolved concerns about its wrongful use for employment purposes.

We again approached majority leader Burton Barr and requested an examination of University of Arizona transfer credit policies.

> *Ratings given by AACRAO are intended to reflect opinion and practice of only one school, but they are often accepted without question by many other schools. It is also common for an admissions officer in one state to contact the reporting officer or acquaintance in another state to determine what their practice is in regard to transferring credits from a school in that state. As reported in the AACRAO guide, the University of Arizona rates credits from University of Phoenix as not acceptable. Since this rating has been adopted by schools in other states as well, credits from University of Phoenix will generally not be accepted by schools throughout the state. Reliance by other states on the guide. . . . mean[s] that schools in other states will adopt a policy of not accepting University of Phoenix credits.*[62]

The report brought no respite from the University of Arizona policy toward the University of Phoenix, so I drafted transfer-credit legislation and found plenty of willing sponsors in the Arizona legislature.

> *Prescribe that the institutions [state universities] . . . evaluate, without prejudice, applicants for admission from regionally accredited postsecondary institutions . . . on the individual merits of their academic achievements and individual capability to complete the courses and the curriculum requirements.*[63]

The University of Arizona tried to vitiate the need for the legislation by rescinding its transfer degree and credit policies toward all accredited institutions in Arizona. This cynical action failed to solve the problem with a legislature intent on passing the University of Phoenix bill and the regents requested a meeting.

> *After two hours of acrimonious argument, and only after Mr. Barr assured them we had the votes [to pass the UOP legislation], did they capitulate and agree to adopt the language of the bill as Regental policy.*[64]

John Sperling, Dino DeConcini, and I rode in Dino's yellow Chevelle convertible back to our offices. I allowed that I felt like a Native American who had just signed yet another treaty with the United States Army Cavalry.

State universities honored the policy more in the breach than in the observance, but with the continued scrutiny of now many supportive legislators, only occasionally did a University of Phoenix student or graduate complain about ill treatment.

Other matters were hotly afoot.

CHAPTER

12

Forces Within/Forces Without

Peter Ellis worked with the Community Schools Program through the San Jose State School of Education and joined forces with John Sperling in the field-testing of off-campus courses for working adults. Following Sperling's meeting at San Jose State, where he was reminded that it would take years to obtain approval for innovative programs, Peter had encouraged John to seek out private institutions.

Following a successful visit to the University of San Francisco with a new president brought in to address declining enrollments, John and his two fellow shareholders Ellis and Crawford incorporated what became IPD. In recognition of Ellis's primary management role, John agreed to rewrite the IPD shareholders' agreement to give Peter the right to buy shares sufficient for majority control of the company if he sold any of his shares. John inserted a provision that required the IPD Corporation to agree to the transfer of shares between shareholders, and since he owned the majority of shares, he believed he controlled his fate.

John's creation of the University of Phoenix with its toxic political and regulatory problems led Peter to perceive—very realistically—it was doomed and destined to bring IPD down with it. John sought to create a holding company to own IPD and the University of Phoenix and learned that the phrase *Notwithstanding anything to the contrary in the Agreement*[65] constituted a virus that would trigger Ellis's right to purchase a majority of shares in the company.

Sperling's reasons for creating a holding company were eminently practical.

> *It was not until the University was accredited by the North Central Association that I became aware of the "change of ownership or change of control issue." In such an event, an institution's accreditation is automatically terminated and had to be reinstated. Additionally, most state licensing agencies had the same stipulation, and more important, so did the U.S. Department of Education. In the latter instance, an institution's eligibility for federally insured student loans terminated and it would take six months to a year to get it reinstated. My solution was to create Apollo Group, a holding company that would own 100 percent of University of Phoenix in perpetuity and thus protect it from regulatory harm.*[66]

Ellis would support the plan if he received a six-year, no-cut contract, the right to buy back shares he had to sell because of the terms of a divorce settlement, and enough proxy votes to ensure that he and his allies would have the same percentage representation on the board of the holding company.[67] John refused and Peter countered with an offer to sell his 13 percent of the company for one million dollars.

Given the desperate financial state of the University of Phoenix and IPD, John rejected the proposal. The University of Phoenix law firm devised a solution through the creation of a new University of Phoenix corporate entity to replace the existing one. If this action were taken, the virus would die.

Thurston Manning, executive director of the commission, determined prospectively, and then officially, that the management, board, and shareholders of the new corporate entity remained materially the same as the original University of Phoenix corporate entity after the transfer of shares from the old to the new, and accreditation would continue.

State licensing agencies followed North Central's lead. There was no accreditation hiatus, and eligibility for federally guaranteed student loans continued uninterrupted. Peter accepted a buyout based on a Price-Waterhouse valuation and John Sperling created the Apollo Group.

Mystifying Disappearance of the "Three Little Words"

Shortly after the reenactment of the California Private Postsecondary Education Act—governing the licensure of private postsecondary institutions—and only months after the university had established operations in California by virtue of WASC forcing the end of IPD's California contracts and now being accredited, a clandestine meeting was held in the Sacramento state capitol that included the consultant to the Assembly Education Committee, Bill Chavez, an aide to a state senator who was carrying a "cleanup" bill to address technical problems with the part of the reenacted law affecting non academic career schools, and unidentified individuals from the California higher education establishment.

Ordinarily, technical cleanup legislation doesn't contain policy changes that require committee analysis, legislative debate, public notice or discussion, and typically passes pro forma.

Unidentified representatives of the California higher education establishment, the legislative aide, and the committee consultant colluded to covertly eliminate the statutory language governing the licensure of accredited out-of-state colleges and universities. Without the knowledge of the legislature and the governor, they would end California's recognition of regional accreditation other than that of WASC for state licensure.

This covert action was taken because University of Phoenix accreditation qualified it for automatic California licensure.

Based on the behavior of the California higher education establishment defending the covert change, it is not far-fetched to conclude that participants were fully aware of what they were doing when they concealed the elimination of a major higher education policy in a career school technical cleanup bill. They believed they committed no sin despite consciously violating one of the California legislature's most time-honored operating rules.

Feverish, but ultimately failed efforts were undertaken by WASC, California Postsecondary Education Commission staff, and the Association of Independent California Colleges and Universities to divine a procedure for the accreditation of the California programs of out-of-state institutions that would be acceptable to the Council on Postsecondary Accreditation (COPA).

The back room cabal resulted in the three words *or applicable regional* being deleted from the section of the law governing the licensure of out-of-state accredited institutions; only WASC-accredited institutions qualified for automatic state licensure. Elimination of the "three little words" was concealed from virtually all members of the legislature and their legislative staff, and even the governor. The statute containing the term, "or applicable regional," honored a longstanding national policy of reciprocity among regional accrediting associations and state licensure agencies.

It was recognized nationally that accreditation was more rigorous than state licensure, and reciprocity frees colleges and universities from spending time and money to complete a redundant licensing process.

The covert elimination of reciprocity—by design and intent—received no committee analysis, no public notice or discussion, passed the California assembly and senate without comment or debate, and was signed into law by the governor. As intended, it went unnoticed by accredited out-of-state colleges and universities.

It even went undetected by the California Office of Legislative Counsel mandated by law to produce an exegesis of all bills enacted by the legislature.

Out-of-state accredited colleges and universities were tersely informed they had two years to get degree programs offered in California WASC accredited; obtain state approval for each degree program, or acquire licenses as a nonaccredited degree-granting institutions in the diploma mill category profiled in the *60 Minutes* exposé. California's higher education powers-that-be—candidly acknowledging awareness of the policy change—adamantly denied responsibility for covertly deleting it.

They defended it savagely.

Casting themselves as paragons of educational probity, the higher education establishment asserted that California should exercise control over all higher education institutions operating within its boundaries. Probity so defined was a dangerous precedent for not only accredited out-of-state colleges and universities, but for the integrity of the legislative process.

The University of Phoenix didn't fantasize its claim about WASC prejudice:

> *We had some serious questions about the quality of the degrees offered through Sperling's program, said Kay Anderson, head of the association (WASC). He said that if University of Phoenix were located at California, it would probably be denied accreditation.*[68]

The practical choice was to apply for licensure as a nonaccredited academic degree-granting institution in the diploma mill licensure category.

Our California critics believed it was precisely where we belonged.

We possessed a more controversial option, legislation to reinstate accreditation reciprocity. Accredited out-of-state colleges and universities had two years to come into compliance, and my first task was to ascertain how WASC intended to interpret the law. I also had to determine whether it was acting within the scope of its recognition by the Council on Postsecondary Accreditation.

WASC readily established procedures to accredit the California programs of accredited out-of-state colleges and universities. WASC procedures appeared to confirm—because of its centrality and alacrity in its implementation—it possessed prior knowledge of the covert repeal. WASC board and senior commission members were well placed in California's public and private colleges and universities, and it is not unrealistic to infer they too possessed prior knowledge.

Given its far-reaching consequences, it seems unlikely it could have been made without the de facto agreement or participation of the postsecondary commission staff who went to often apoplectic lengths to publicly defend its covert elimination.

WASC "accredited" programs of five out-of-state institutions. By accrediting programs rather than institutions, I believed these "accreditations" evidenced that WASC exceeded the scope of its recognition by the Council on Postsecondary Accreditation. WASC did not have the authority to grant accreditation for individual degree programs in its own region much less those in their region offered by institutions accredited by other regional associations.

Almost after two years of hollow foot-dragging following WASC "accreditation" of the programs offered by five public out-of-state colleges and universities, the Council on Postsecondary Accreditation begrudgingly notified WASC their programmatic accrediting actions exceeded the scope of their accrediting authority.

WASC program "accreditation" was worthless if not fraudulent.

Between the period of time when WASC published procedures for "accreditation" of out-of-state institutions programs, and program accreditation was deemed outside its authority, it changed its interpretation of the California Postsecondary Education Act multiple times. After COPA notice that it exceeded the scope of its recognition, WASC unilaterally renamed its programmatic accreditation "certification."

We requested an attorney general's opinion about the meaning of the term "accreditation" contained in the California Private Postsecondary Education Act.

The attorney general determined that the reenacted Private Postsecondary Act required WASC accreditation, not certification. WASC rescinded its programmatic accreditation role. The covert policy change was inoperable.

All accredited out-of-state institutions, if they wished to remain in California, were forced into a licensure category with California's unaccredited diploma mills.

If the reciprocity termination had not occurred covertly in a career school cleanup bill, its illegality and inoperability would have been identified. The change received no analysis or public hearing, so its legal and operational disabilities went unidentified and unaddressed with unmerited consequences to accredited out-of-state institutions and their thousands of California students.

During the time of the legislative enactment of the bill that eliminated accreditation reciprocity—in a transparent effort to legislate market share by eliminating competition—the legislature enacted a bill that provided that persons seeking teacher certification would only be allowed to enroll in degree programs provided by WASC-accredited institutions.

WASC-accredited colleges and universities were either unwilling or unable to meet the need for teacher education, and tens of thousands of uncertified teachers were working in California's K-12 schools—almost without exception in poorer districts, because there were not enough degree programs offered by WASC accredited schools to qualify them for state certification.

It was reported subsequently that the assembly member who carried the market-share legislation for the California higher education establishment falsely claimed to have earned a degree from the University of California at Berkeley.

CHAPTER

13

"Egregious" College

There does not exist a more baroque example of academic disingenuousness, institutional delusion, fabricated high dudgeon, moral dissembling, and general prickliness than the experience IPD had with Regis College of Denver, Colorado (now Regis University).

The legal victory and resulting financial damages literally saved Apollo Group, IPD, and the University of Phoenix from bankruptcy. The degree of avaricious stoop and moral expediency evidenced by some Regis personnel has not been recognized by those only believing or acquainted with Regis's ornate distortions of the shameful episode.

I nicknamed Regis, "Egregious" College.

Regis/IPD Contract

Regis, like other IPD contract institutions, experienced an enrollment decline among traditional-aged students, and needed adult students or it could fold. Eighteen months later, the Regis/IPD programs enrolled nearly twelve hundred working adult students. By measures financial and educational, it was a home run.

IPD saved Regis from closure.

The Butterball Effect again materialized, this time on an arid, sleepy, sparsely populated Denver campus.

Regis charged IPD with breach of contract.

> *The news from Regis was a shock for several reasons—our cash flow was still precarious, the Phoenix newspapers were certain to seize on the news and give it maximum publicity, and, if Regis was successful, the other IPD contract institutions would very likely follow suit with bankruptcy almost certain. This was major trouble.*[69]

A Denver law firm represented IPD in a dangerously expensive, stressful, and seemingly endless forty-two-month slog through the political, factual, and legal firmament of contract law. IPD's lawyer immediately contacted Regis College—Regis refused to meet with IPD after the breach notice—and a sit down was arranged with the dean responsible for the administration of the contract.

> *[John Sperling]"Just tell us what to do and we'll do it."*
>
> *[The dean] refused to do it unless I admitted the breach, a thing I was not about to do.*[70]

Counsel ordered IPD to maintain clean hands. This meant IPD had to underwrite the cost of implementing the contract even though it was certain Regis would terminate it. IPD filed a request for a temporary restraining order and preliminary injunction.

> *[The judge] refused the temporary restraining order and preliminary injunction but ruled that we had justiciable issues with an adequate remedy in law. Ominously, [the judge] added an obiter dictum, "This is certainly no judgment, but as I read the contract, the parties agreed to vest Regis with sole discretion." Regis took this as confirmation of its right to act as it wished and immediately sent IPD a notice of termination.* [71]

Turning yet another misfortune into an opportunity, the Colorado IPD sign was replaced with a University of Phoenix sign. Like the losses of contracts in California, Regis's termination provided the University of Phoenix with experienced staff eager to go head to head with local colleges and universities. Colorado law recognized University of Phoenix's accreditation for licensure.

Shortly after the contract termination, John Sperling dropped the entire Regis matter in my lap. There were thousands of contract documents about which I knew nothing. We didn't have funds for lawyers to determine factual bases of the breach allegations, so I was tasked with making sense out of how IPD fulfilled the contract to determine if a dangerously expensive lawsuit was warranted. I had to verify to what extent, if any, the breach allegations were true.

According to Regis College, IPD

- Failed to maintain current academic records and information on students enrolling in the program including inaccurate class lists and student registration information,
- Violated the "Student Tuition and Fees" agreement by permitting students who had not paid to

participate in classes and allowing students to postdate checks,

- Improperly assigned its rights and/or obligations under the agreement to University of Phoenix and/or other entities without prior written consent,
- Failed to adhere to "North Central marketing standards" by allowing an IPD student representative on at least one occasion to state that Regis was going to raise prices and had cash flow problems,
- Violated a site-approval provision by offering courses at sites not approved by Regis, and
- Failed to observe the Regis grading system.[72]

Interviews with IPD staff revealed some issues related to alleged breaches surfaced during the eighteen months the contract was operative, but were always resolved to Regis's apparent satisfaction. I drilled down into thousands of potential trial exhibits and uncovered a treasure trove in the records maintained by the IPD contract director who obsessively documented virtually every interaction related to his administration of the contract.

A deeply troubling picture soon emerged of Regis's financially self-aggrandizing manufacture of distortions and falsehoods used to justify the contract termination. Regis's ethical behavior mirrored our Arizona and California higher education opponents.

The Butterball Effect was in full flower.

Welcome to the Rocky Mountain state.

Breach 1: Student Records

Regis alleged course registration cards were not provided after the first class as required. Regis policy allowed students to miss the first class, and so no attendance, no registration card. Regis experienced the same problem following the contract termination. It made instructors responsible for collecting registration cards and imposed delayed payment of salaries to enforce the responsibility. IPD could not have ordered faculty to collect registration cards—or employed sanctions—because they were employed and supervised by Regis.

Breach 2: Student Tuition Collections

The problem with "student tuition collections" arose solely from Regis policies. Policy was to collect tuition at the first class, but was contravened by other policies and practices: students were allowed to miss the first night of class, some employers paid tuition, and tuition was underwritten by a variety of student aid programs.

Breach 3: Assignment of Contract Rights

This was based on a Regis dean's glance at an Apollo Group letterhead that listed the Institute for Professional Development and the University of Phoenix as subsidiaries.

Breach 4: Violation of North Central Marketing Standards

Regis claimed IPD violated a North Central marketing standard because of the sole instance when an unidentified student allegedly made the comment in class that Regis was "raising prices and had a cash flow problem."

Breach 5: Approval of Class Sites

Three sites offered classes without Regis's approval the date IPD was declared in breach. There was one reason for the apparent violation; Regis never made one class site inspection or once granted approval. It relied on the Veteran's Administration to do it. All three had been approved by the Veteran's Administration prior to the contract termination by Regis.

Breach 6: Use of Improper Grading System
IPD was responsible for hiring and training of faculty in Regis's academic policies, but once IPD exercised this responsibility, control passed to Regis.

Federal Trial

Based on my documentation of IPD's implementation of the contract, I recommended to John Sperling that we pursue legal recourse and he agreed. We believed IPD would get more "home-towned" by a Denver jury sympathetic to Regis College's efforts to free itself from a for-profit higher education company than from a judge, and decided on a bench trial. Regis believed it was going to clean our clocks no matter who heard the case and agreed to trial by judge rather than by jury.

The federal court trial was held in Denver before Judge John P. Moore, a Regis College graduate.

It was immediately evident that the Regis attorney did not remotely approach our meticulousness in trial preparation. He was archly dismissive of the hundreds of exhibits evidencing IPD had not breached the contract. Regis's lawyer predicated his defense of Regis on the written comment made by the superior court judge denying IPD's injunction. The gratuitous comment—which the judge qualified as not a legal opinion—indicated that Regis appeared to have *sole discretion* in interpreting the contract.

Sole discretion proved to be a poorly engineered linchpin in defense of Regis's revocation of the IPD contract.

IPD's lawyer comprehensively documented that breaches alleged by Regis were factually baseless or resulted solely from Regis's policies and management practices. The contract also guaranteed the breaching party the opportunity to correct all breaches, but Regis refused to inform IPD of what it wanted done to correct the breaches, even after John Sperling offered: *"Just tell us what to do, and we'll do it."*

Early in the trial, Judge Moore ruled categorically against Regis's sole-discretion argument. Regis's attorney persisted in restating it and was admonished repeatedly. Moore became so exasperated that whenever the Regis lawyer commenced one of his racking sole-discretion perorations, he literally turned his high-backed leather chair toward the wall behind the bench so all any of us could see was the top of his head.

The Regis attorney finally reached the point of apparent blind desperation, where he would strut to the lectern, extend his arms and anchor his hands on it, then generate and hold an expression the uninformed might mistake for someone in profound thought.

John Sperling and I were optimistic about the trial outcome. Despite our belief, IPD counsel persuaded John to make a settlement offer. John was reluctant, but our lawyer's legal acumen and courtroom performance had proven exemplary, so he agreed. The offer to settle for one million dollars was instantly rejected by Regis.

Judge Moore adjourned the trial and set the date for findings and ruling some three weeks hence. IPD expended nearly $300,000 in legal fees and costs over three years when finances were a critical daily issue. Based on the contract record analysis and the legal conclusions expressed by our attorney, we had rolled the dice.

If we didn't win a substantial settlement, Apollo, IPD, and the University of Phoenix faced bankruptcy. We were obviously wound tight when Judge Moore reconvened the trial.

> *In my judgment, there are two matters which are fundamental here. First, the contract contained very specific conditions regarding the right of termination, not the least of which was a provision giving the alleged breaching party the right to cure the breach within 30 days of the breach notice. Second, it is uncontroverted in my eyes that by its conduct Regis effectively deprived IPD of its contractual right to cure the alleged breaches. Indeed, both the breach allegations and the conduct of certain Regis personnel display a pettiness which I find shocking in an institution with the reputation of Regis College.*[73]

Sole discretion would be entombed forever in Regis's academic grove.

> *I have witnessed from certain quarters attitudes of myopia and dogmatism which doubtlessly fostered this litigation. These attitudes surfaced in the initiation of staff complaints about the alleged breaches, sustained during the period between the notice of the breach and termination, and flowered during the litigation. In my opinion, the undercurrent attitude was a total hindrance to any responsible resolution to the problems wrought in this case.*[74]

Judge Moore's finding of facts cut to the bone of the alleged breaches:

> **Student Records:** *[I] find that there was indeed a problem with class registrations, but the problem was not caused by IPD's failure to maintain adequate records.*
>
> **Student Tuition Collections:** *It did not exist on December 31, 1981 [the date Regis declared IPD in breach of contract].*
>
> **Assignment of Contract Rights:** *Of all the alleged breaches, this is the most specious.*
>
> **Violation of North Central Standards:** *This alleged breach can be described as both petty and specious.*
>
> **Approval of Class Sites:** *[I] conclude that this alleged breach did not constitute a basis for termination . . . because it had been corrected long prior to December 31, 1981.*
>
> **Use of Improper Grading System:** *IPD had no control over the grades given by any instructor, nor did it have the practical means for correcting the grading errors of any instructor. Accordingly, I conclude that IPD did not breach . . . nor did such a breach exist on December 31, 1981.*[75]

A settlement hearing established financial damages and attorney's fees totaling $1.95 million that Regis paid over a three-year period. The influx of some $650,000 per year that dropped to the bottom line kept Apollo Group, the University of Phoenix, and IPD financially viable during an otherwise financially desperate time (during that period we let some 40 percent of University of Phoenix staff go).

The University of Phoenix flourished in Colorado and would probably not have been established without

The Butterball Effect manifested by Regis College. Regis terminated the IPD contract, and not only guaranteed the economic survival of IPD, but the University of Phoenix and Apollo Group.

A few years later, The *Wall Street Journal* published a front-page story about the Regis College extended learning system for working adults with sole credit for its creation, innovative components, and implementation arrogated by its president without mention of IPD.

Out of the blue a few more years later, an on-campus Regis student reporter was referred to me to get an opinion on a story that had gained a life of its own: the IPD contract was terminated because it was turning Regis into a diploma mill.

The objective account of Regis/IPD contract dispute was contained in Judge John Moore's order in *IPD v Regis College*. I sent the reporter a copy.

I contacted him later to inquire if he ever wrote his story on how Regis preserved its academic integrity.

"There are more important things to write about at Regis College!"

CHAPTER

14

California Political Theater

Notification by the California Office of Private Postsecondary Education that University of Phoenix accreditation would no longer satisfy licensure requirements, and accredited out-of-state colleges and universities would be required to be accredited by WASC, have degree programs licensed individually by the State of California, or be licensed by the state as a nonaccredited degree-granting institution, would make the political battle in Arizona a Three Stooges swordfight with celery sticks.

The University of Phoenix was viewed in California as a sinister outlier because it was portrayed by WASC, the postsecondary commission staff, and the Association of Independent California Colleges and Universities, as an institution whose founder was driven out of California because of the "questionable" quality of education delivered through IPD contracts with WASC-accredited schools.

Once these contracts terminated, the California higher education establishment appeared unconcerned that the contract institutions retained virtually all IPD's innovations.

The higher education establishment's depiction of John Sperling was that he had evaporated into Arizona because it didn't have diploma mill laws where he could obtain accreditation from a regional association with no standards. An oversight in California law permitted Sperling's new institution to be recognized with the same status as WASC-accredited institutions.

Barefacedly, despite the shadowy depiction of John Sperling, IPD, and the University of Phoenix, the newly reenacted private postsecondary act statutorily guaranteed that the California licensure of institutions like those profiled in the *60 Minutes* expose maintained their franchises to sell the Great Seal of the State of California in the form of phony college degrees.

Persons unfamiliar with accreditation often think state licensure is identical and foreign nationals from countries where the government solely regulates higher education believed bogus degrees sold by California-licensed institutions were authentic.

California State Capitol Free Fire Zone

The first step after notification that we had to be accredited by WASC or be licensed as an unaccredited institution was to hire someone in Sacramento familiar with education politics and acquainted personally with key higher education players in the California legislature. We could not afford a full-time lobbyist and had two years to be relicensed. I'd have to resolve the problem any way I could.

Dr. Joseph Maloney was a Mott Fellow with Peter Ellis at the University of Michigan School of Education employed by the California State Department of Education.

Joe, a former Sacramento high school teacher, subsequently headed a civics education foundation for K-12 students and coordinated statewide programs with the criminal justice system, so he always worked for us part time. Our first task was to determine how California's reciprocity policy got eliminated.

A senator's aide shrugged his shoulders when asked about how accreditation reciprocity disappeared in his boss's vocational school cleanup bill.

Jim Browne, the veteran consultant to the Senate Education Committee, was adamant that he knew nothing about how the surreptitious policy change transpired.

The consultant to the Assembly Education Committee, Bill Chavez, threw his hands in the air.

The mystification of the staff insiders was infrangible.

Chavez and Browne were openly skeptical of the University of Phoenix because it was in the political crosshairs of the California higher education establishment. I started from scratch educating them about our teaching/learning model for working adults, of which they either knew little, or possessed distorted perceptions.

I had to establish credibility, and when doing so could never misspeak, misstate, exaggerate, hedge, angle, embellish, or obscure anything; even one unconscious remark could be trumpeted into a raging political problem. Key to this trying process was establishing the legitimacy and recognition of the working adult learner. Once that was accomplished, the University of Phoenix model for the degree education of working adults would start to make sense.

Joe and I gained credibility with Chavez and Browne. They were basic to restoration of reciprocity because they analyzed and explained legislation and policies for the members of the assembly and senate education committees. In the weeks that followed, our relationship with them continued to improve. Chavez was willing to discuss reciprocity with the chair of the Assembly Education Committee.

We set a meeting.

Joe and I entered Chavez's office that Monday morning and his anger was blistering. A lieutenant governor's aide had barnstormed him and allegedly ordered him to do the University of Phoenix's political bidding. The aide reportedly did the same thing to the chair of the committee, an alleged protégée of the lieutenant governor. I told Chavez I knew nothing about it and it was obviously something I would have never approved. Our relationship never recovered. In the tiny community of Sacramento state capital politics, whatever credibility Joe and I had established had just been obliterated.

We were not only back to square one; we were off the game board.

Unknown to me, Sperling apparently requested the political sting from the lieutenant governor. The half-baked meddling intensified and lengthened the political fight and ridiculously spiked the cost of the battle. Word spread instantly. Whatever foothold Joe and I gained through exposure of a backroom conspiracy to change California law without legislative knowledge didn't matter; some "sleazy out-of-state diploma mill" tried to politically shake down the Assembly Education Committee.

For a dreadfully long, excruciatingly painful, and depressing period of time after that event, I was treated in the California capitol as if I was a lobbyist for the North American Man-Boy Love Association at a plenary session of fundamentalist Christians, Association for the Preservation of the Nuclear Family, Doomsday Preppers, State of Texas secessionists, the Federalist Society, and the American Federation for the Protection of Large Clip Family Room Assault Rifles.

Sperling and I were friends with John Vasconcellos, chair of the Assembly Permanent Subcommittee on Postsecondary Education, and explored the possibility of him carrying a bill to restore reciprocity. Vasconcellos, also friends with the executive director of the postsecondary commission, would remain neutral. He introduced a "spot bill" with a number, but no content. We would have to find an author.

Visit to WASC

Vasconcellos convened a meeting with representatives of the postsecondary commission and the Association of Independent California Colleges and Universities with Joe and me in a sincere attempt to mediate the conflict. Despite chapter and verse about WASC enmity toward the University of Phoenix and IPD, the response was "how do you know you won't get accredited unless you try?"

Vasconcellos prevailed upon me personally to meet with WASC.

WASC Senior Commission office was a terra-cotta-roofed, Spanish mission-style house at Mills College in Oakland, California. Dr. Jim Miklich, University of Phoenix executive vice president, and I were bemused that the headquarters of the entity that caused both IPD and the

University of Phoenix such irksome problems resembled a cozy and exclusive country clinic of cool purpose.

The WASC senior commission executive director and assistant director were antiseptically cordial in answering questions about their latest revision of the process they repeatedly crafted for the "accreditation" of the California programs of accredited out-of-state institutions.

I inquired if WASC was capable of conducting an objective evaluation of the University of Phoenix.

The executive director ardently pooh-poohed prejudice toward any institution—especially one as lowly as University of Phoenix—and praised the integrity of WASC accreditation evaluations and the highly respected California academics who participated in an honorable and aboveboard process.

I asked about his statement reported in the *Arizona Republic* that the University of Phoenix would *probably be denied accreditation.*

A secretary ushered us out in silence.

Because of political problems arising from the attempt to strong-arm the consultant and chair of the Assembly Education Committee, no legislator we approached to carry a bill would have anything to do with it. Sperling obtained a connection with former California Governor, the late Pat Brown. The affable politician of the old school was the father of recently reelected—thirty-six years after being first elected governor—Jerry Brown. Sperling retained Pat Brown with the idea of forming a California advisory board. I tug-boated him around the capitol to meet with legislators.

Sam Farr, a young assembly member from Monterey County, agreed to carry our bill.

Our meetings with Assembly Education Committee members did not bode well for its passage even out of the committee of origin. Joe Maloney knew the former chief consultant to the Senate Finance Committee, Jack Watson, who possessed years of hardball experience in Sacramento state capitol politics. Joe and I explained our dilemma and counseled with him on what might be done.

Watson recommended we hire a new lobbying firm, Governmental Advocates.

Governmental Advocates

Governmental Advocates consisted of a brilliant, power-packed, politically effective with both political parties, and dramatically beautiful single mother of two boys named Hedy Govenar, and Jerry Zanelli, the former chief executive officer of the Senate Rules Committee.

Zanelli was politically wily, deeply experienced, and physically massive. If Hedy stood behind him, it was impossible to see her.

We candidly explained the political history of the University of Phoenix, the disappearance of the "three little words," and the poisoned political atmosphere arising from the barnstorming the chair and consultant of the Assembly Education Committee.

They would check us out.

Most from whom Hedy and Jerry obtained reaction to the prospect of representing the University of Phoenix—the postsecondary commission, the Association of Independent California Colleges and Universities, other lobbyists, legislators and their staffs—went ballistic. Some warned they would be forced out of business and others angrily threatened to put them out of business. Why would they ever represent a diploma mill?

The response of the California higher education establishment was so astonishingly hostile, that the political fight was irresistible. Hedy and Jerry's temperament fit perfectly with John Sperling and me. I detailed the political facts of life at the California state capitol to Sperling.

He would find the funds to hire Governmental Advocates.

State Capitol Media Hurricane

Ten days after Hedy and Jerry registered as University of Phoenix lobbyists, incendiary articles and columns appeared in the *Sacramento Bee* and *Sacramento Union,* the *San Francisco Examiner*, and even the *Arizona Republic.* Almost overnight, the fight with the California higher education establishment had become pitilessly public.

The only thing correct in any of the stories or columns was the spelling of University of Phoenix. Our bill simply called for a moratorium on California's elimination of accreditation reciprocity so that the postsecondary commission could complete a study on it. Typical of many in traditional higher education who besieged the University of Phoenix, the political reaction was spectacularly out of scale to the actual proposal.

The column by Dan Walters in the *Sacramento Union* newspaper crystallized the distortions about the University of Phoenix that had appeared in the Arizona media and took things to new historical and political heights of make-believe.

The convolution of falsehoods and misperceptions had been derived—according to Walters's deposition testimony in a libel lawsuit brought by the University of Phoenix against the *Sacramento Union*—from meetings with the postsecondary commission's governmental affairs officer, Suzanne Ness.[76]

A couple of years ago, the California legislature enacted a new body of law aimed at curbing the proliferation of so-called "diploma mills" that sell impressive-sounding educational degrees without offering real education.[77]

Outrageously contrary to postsecondary commission claims about going after "diploma mills," the reenactment of the postsecondary education act statutorily guaranteed that the California diploma mills profiled in the CBS *60 Minutes* expose could freely continue to exploit their licenses to sell degrees under color of state authority.

In addition to the more than a hundred unaccredited degree-granting entities holding valid state licenses—following reenactment of the California private postsecondary licensing law—virtually anyone who invested $50,000 and completed an application could still buy the right to print degrees symbolically affixed with the Great Seal of the State of California.

The postsecondary commission affirmed the retention of the code section used to license California's diploma mills by engineering it in the reenactment of the postsecondary act. Walter's explanation of the reenactment was deeply flawed in accuracy but not impact.

The law required, in brief, that degree-issuing institutions acquire accreditation by recognized organizations, primarily the Western Association of Schools and Colleges. It was estimated that about 30 institutions in California would be affected by the law. All but one of them either complied or went out of business.

The single exception was University of Phoenix.[78]

Walters claimed all higher education institutions operating in California had to be WASC accredited, which was untrue. Anyone holding a state license was still selling bogus degrees and WASC program accreditation was worthless. Walters—under the political tutelage of the postsecondary commission staff—inaccurately transformed California's shameless problems with state licensed, unaccredited diploma mills, into consummately fabricated problems with accredited out–of-state colleges and universities.

Five accredited out-of-state colleges and universities—all public institutions—were granted ultimately fraudulent WASC program accreditation, and the rest, including the University of Phoenix, obtained licensure in the nonaccredited institutional category.

Following his tortured convolution of fact and fiction, Walters took an even more destructive path in the distortion of both the California and Arizona political history of the University of Phoenix.

> *Arizona does not regulate private, degree granting colleges and has been described as a Mecca for questionable diploma mills. Pro-regulation forces in Arizona have described Sperling . . . as [a] major obstacle[s] to anti-diploma mill legislation in the state. Those considerable talents did not prevent the California Legislature from enacting fairly tough anti-diploma mill laws in 1981.*[79]

The University of Phoenix did not take a position for or against the reenactment of the California postsecondary licensing law because reciprocity was retained until underhandedly eliminated. There were no diploma mills in Arizona either before or after the board of regents was prevented from monopolizing both public and private higher education. The reenacted law ensured that the California diploma mill licenses remained lewdly valid.

> *Rather than comply with the new California law . . . University of Phoenix hired some lobbyists . . . to get around the law. State education officials see in the bill the creation of a giant loophole through which diploma mills from throughout the nation could pour into California and set up operations.*[80]

Walters made it appear that Arizona's illusory diploma mills were posed to flood California, but more than a hundred nonaccredited degree-granting institutions of the ilk profiled in the *60 Minutes* expose were still thriving monetarily with valid State of California licenses.

Diploma mills weren't flooding; they were flourishing.

A postsecondary commission staff member apparently convinced Walters that California's problem wasn't with diploma mills endorsed by the postsecondary commission to prosper under color of state authority, but with institutions accredited by an identical type of recognized regional accrediting association as WASC.

A ingenuous member of the news media had been manipulated into authoring—although cunning in its twisting of the issue—a lethal attack on the University of Phoenix.

Members of the California legislature, like their Arizona counterparts, knew virtually nothing about accreditation, state licensure, or the University of Phoenix, other than allegedly being a diploma mill. We faced a crushing political and public relations challenge of nightmarish proportions and pulled our legislation.

Hedy, Jerry, Joe, and I would be back the next legislative session.

CHAPTER

15

Golden State Legislative Fight

Newspaper articles with association of diploma mills and the University of Phoenix continued to find ready currency among many California legislators.

> *A bill has surfaced in California that would allow an Arizona-based alternative college backed by former Gov. Pat Brown to continue its operations in California. Under legislation already enacted aimed at so-called diploma mills which offer degrees with little or no study, University of Phoenix would have been forced to leave California on July 1. Suzanne Ness, a government affairs officer with the CPEC said . . . that Mervyn Dymally's . . . presence has been felt in Sacramento.*[81]

For a California postsecondary commission staff member to mislead the public and the legislature on a major policy issue was disgraceful, particularly when the commission ensured that California's diploma mills could continue to sell phony degrees endorsed by the State of California. Accreditation is barely understood by many in higher education, and, from painful experience, we knew that the likelihood of being able to explain it to California legislators was slim and none.

> *"If this bill passes, it will once again make California a haven for every diploma mill in the nation," said Author E. Hughes, president of the University of San Diego and president of the statewide Association of Independent California Colleges and Universities [AICCU]. "At a time when California is trying to improve the standards of all its education, it is wrong to open the state to every campus in the nation," said Pat Callan, executive director of the California Postsecondary Education Commission.*
>
> *"What happens," said Pat Callan . . ."is that a college or university simply goes to that area where they can get accredited the easiest. They then use that accreditation to come into the lucrative California market and other states and sell themselves on an equal basis with the colleges that have met much more rigorous standards."* [82]

The Association of Independent California Colleges and Universities did not oppose the reenactment of the law that allowed existing diploma mills to continue to operate, and retained the provision that anyone with $50,000 could still obtain a license to sell degrees, yet its president claimed a University of Phoenix bill that called for a licensure study would permit diploma mills to flourish. The executive director of the postsecondary commission memorialized his ignorance about institutional accreditation and transparent contempt for the people who voluntarily participate in its processes.

Creating a Unified Front

The University of Phoenix was singled out as the only institution "trying to get around the law," but there were twenty some other accredited out-of-state colleges and universities providing degree programs in California.

Similar to when we were the target of the Arizona regents and I helped found the Independent Colleges and Universities of Arizona, I created another association, Accredited Out-of-State Colleges and Universities in California (AOCUC): American College for the Applied Arts, Antioch University, City University, Nova University, Union for Experimenting Colleges and Universities (subsequently "Union Institute"), University of Phoenix, College of St. Thomas, and Webster University.

AOCUC Political Action

Colloquies were held by AOCUC representatives with staffs of the postsecondary commission, pro tem of the senate, speaker of the assembly, department of education, senate finance committee, senate and assembly education committees, office of private postsecondary education, superintendent of public instruction, and the Association of Independent California Colleges and Universities.

Painstakingly, AOCUC became proactive—although demonstrably unwanted—participants in the legislative politics of California higher education. We were provided an entertaining decoding of the California Education Code in a California attorney general's opinion:

"(L)arge parts of the Education Code are not meant to be understood." [83]

At the direction of Governmental Advocates, now also representing AOCUC, we visited legislators, their staffs, and committee consultants to seek their support for legislation to restore reciprocity. Key members of the legislature visited California operations of out-of-state institutions and met faculty and students. Students and employers contacted their respective legislators to inform them about their experience with the out-of-state programs.

Reciprocity Legislation

From his days as chief executive officer of the Senate Rules Committee, Jerry Zanelli at Governmental Advocates knew the senator whose career schools "cleanup" legislation eliminated reciprocity. The senator informed Zanelli that the policy elimination had been represented as a "technical amendment" and agreed to carry legislation to restore reciprocity.

Senate Education Committee Hearing

The AOCUC reciprocity bill was heard in the Senate Education Committee. Our opponents included the California Postsecondary Education Commission, the Association of Independent California Colleges and Universities, the California Community Colleges, and the Faculty Association of the California State University System.

The senator testified the elimination of reciprocity was represented to him as a technical amendment.

A lobbyist for the Association of Independent California Colleges and Universities archly testified that although the change had been characterized as a "technical amendment," the privileged few with direct knowledge—allegedly including the senator—fully understood that it eliminated accreditation reciprocity.

A lone, slender gray-haired man in the jammed spectator section of the senate hearing room rose and just stood there. Gradually, attention was focused on Jim Browne. The former consultant to the Senate Education Committee now ran an educational foundation. I had no idea he was even in the hearing room.

The committee chair warmly recognized him and he made his way to the foot of the dais.

Browne testified the bill was represented to him, and thus senators on the Education Committee, as solely containing technical amendments, so when they voted for a career school technical cleanup bill, they had no idea they eliminated California's accreditation reciprocity for accredited out-of-state academic degree granting institutions.

This was not how higher education or any policy changes were supposed to be made in the California legislature, and it wasn't a political process that the Association of Independent California Colleges and Universities should defend, particularly publicly.

Out of the breathless silence that gripped the hearing room, a senator called for the question, and the AOCUC reciprocity bill passed unanimously.

Members of the California higher education establishment in the hearing room were pole axed.

Assembly Education Committee

The next stop was the Assembly Education Committee whose chair remained an avowed enemy of the University of Phoenix because of Sperling's hardheaded political interference. Hedy and Jerry reported they confirmed enough votes from the committee members—despite the opposition of the chair—to get the bill passed.

At the hearing, the chair asked if there was any opposition.

The only movement in the room was the recently defeated Republican gubernatorial candidate, Houston Flournoy, shepherded to the dais by a lobbyist for the independent colleges and universities.

Flournoy was employed by University of Southern California (USC) off-campus graduate program in Sacramento and was second in command of the California Republican Party. Flournoy importuned his fellow Republicans and they switched their votes from yea to nay. Without the last-second switch, reciprocity would have been restored.

The California higher education establishment had just created totally unintended political serendipity for AOCUC.

CHAPTER

16

Establishment Taps Out

Prior to its reenactment, the postsecondary commission made a study of the implementation of the California Private Postsecondary Education Act and used it as the rationale for recommending changes to the law. Accredited out-of-state institutions were to be included in the study to ascertain the degree of oversight exercised by their regional accrediting associations and, if warranted, recommend changes to licensure requirements.

The study of the accredited out-of-state institutions was never undertaken, but commission staff still ruthlessly defended the covert elimination of California's accreditation reciprocity policy. The act remained virtually intact for California's state licensed diploma mills.

The postsecondary commission, WASC, and the Association of Independent California Colleges and

Universities had claimed accredited out-of-state colleges and universities in California had no accrediting association oversight; degree programs were questionable, and some had engaged in fraudulent activities. Evidence was contained in a *Los Angeles Times* series published prior to the reenactment on California athletes who were awarded college credits without attending class or completing coursework.

Two accredited out-of-state institutions were identified: Ottawa College (KS) accredited by North Central and Rocky Mountain College (MT) accredited by the Northwest Association. There were also three WASC-accredited institutions: Los Angeles Valley College, California Lutheran College, and El Camino College.[84] The recipients of credits were athletes from UCLA, USC, and seven other WASC-accredited colleges and universities. One hundred and eighty-five certified California teachers acquired fraudulent academic credentials that allowed step increases in their salaries from St. Stephens Educational Bible College, licensed by the State of California.[85]

The postsecondary commission study on the implementation of the postsecondary education act documented written complaints filed with the Office of Private Postsecondary Education against accredited and nonaccredited postsecondary institutions operating in California between 1977 when the act was made law, and 1981 when it was renewed.

Written Complaints

WASC	46	
NATTS[86]	135	
AICS[87]	121	
NHSC[88]	135	
Other Regionals[89]	37	(includes NHSC number for 1982)
Non-accredited[90]	936	
Total	**1,410**	

Postsecondary institutions accredited by WASC, other accrediting entities recognized by the Council on Postsecondary Accreditation, and unaccredited institutions licensed by the State of California constituted nearly all of the complaints. "Other Regionals"—accredited out-of-state colleges and universities—represented the smallest number (this category included an unknown number of complaints against the National Home Study Council).

Despite overwhelming problems with California institutions, including those WASC accredited, the postsecondary commission endorsed the reenactment of the law that permitted California's diploma mills—the overwhelming percentage of complaints—to continue to operate unrestrictedly under color of state authority.

They went after institutions with the least complaints: accredited out-of-state colleges and universities.

Meeting with Chair of Postsecondary Commission

The senator who carried the AOCUC reciprocity bill, together with politically influential coauthors, again agreed to sponsor reciprocity legislation. The opposition, led by the postsecondary commission, remained intransigent.

Due to the nature of a political fight that demands careful attention to legislative details and vote counting, I had assumed—along with everyone else—that postsecondary commission members were in accord with the covert reciprocity policy change and its savage defense by their executive staff. Was the commission actually conversant with staff actions? I sought to meet with the chair, a founder of the postsecondary commission.

Hedy asked the new executive officer of the Senate Rules Committee to invite the chair to a meeting with AOCUC in the rules chamber of the state capitol. Hedy and I entered the anteroom of the chamber to see the distinguished, but bewildered chair of the postsecondary commission, Dr. Stephen Teale, bookended on a tiny bench by its executive director and governmental-affairs officer who crashed our meeting with him.

Moments after we were seated in the chamber, the executive director exploded in a torrent of vituperation toward Hedy, the University of Phoenix, and me. As I recall, he raged something to the effect: "How dare we go around him to a member of his board without his knowledge and permission? How dare we conduct a meeting in the Senate Rules chamber? This is the most underhanded and cynical political manipulation I have ever encountered in all my years at the state capitol. How dare we . . . How . . . !"

The commission chair looked even more bewildered.

I addressed him: "This is not a productive way to commence a meeting on an important higher education issue to the people of California." I explained how California covertly eliminated its longstanding policy of accreditation reciprocity. Because the policy change was made surreptitiously, its legal and operational problems were not identified, and the requirement for WASC programmatic accreditation was inoperable. AOCUC would provide documentation to the commission.

Hedy informed me shortly thereafter that the California Postsecondary Education Commission was ready to compromise.

We were recognized players at the California higher education policy table.

The Compromise

Though cooperating with accredited out-of-state colleges and universities in developing licensure legislation, California higher education powers-that-be remained opposed to reciprocity.

It was politically feasible to reinstate reciprocity, but if so advantaged, when California's market share of accredited out-of-state colleges and universities increased, we remained readily susceptible to political attack. The out-of-state association formed because we shared vulnerability. Without shared vulnerability, participation would erode and disappear.

If there were a licensure category for accredited out-of-state colleges and universities that recognized our accreditation, but mandated a state review, we'd maintain the integrity of our accreditation and silence the critics. We would seek institutional representation—historically accorded to each postsecondary licensure category—on a new private postsecondary licensing council. We'd develop a "safe harbor" through a statutory role in the regulatory apparatus.

The opportunity for WASC and the rest of the California higher education establishment to behave like a trade association would be minimized. I helped ensure the new licensure scenario played out by demanding the restoration of reciprocity. It was the old Br'er Rabbit political conceit:

"Whatever you do, don't throw us in the briar patch."

The postsecondary commission sponsored legislation to create a new regulatory agency, the Council for Private Postsecondary Educational Institutions. Included was a licensure category for accredited out-of-state colleges and universities and representation on the council. Legislation required the commission to establish a committee to develop the standards for out-of-state schools licensure. I was appointed with some allies. The majority of committee members always warmly cradled—talisman-like—the WASC Handbook on Accreditation.

The WASC doppelgangers solemnly pushed a licensure taxonomy for accredited out-of-state colleges and universities that mirrored WASC accreditation nomenclature. They believed WASC accreditation was vastly different from and superior to other regional accreditation. North Central and other accrediting associations observed identical Council On Postsecondary Accreditation criteria.

They did not understand institutional accreditation.

I was appointed the state senate representative of accredited out-of-state institutions on the new council, chaired the committee that developed licensure regulations, and later was elected council chair. All accredited out-of-state institutions completed the new licensure process, and new licensure standards for nonaccredited degree-granting entities resulted in all ceasing operation, leaving the state, or losing their licenses.

One long-existing and infamous California-licensed unaccredited "university" received an evaluation visit by the council that resulted in a denial of licensure recommendation. Prior to the meeting where a vote on the recommendation would be taken, council members were provided documentation by the institution in support of relicensure.

Among the documents was a description of its educational mission.

I had written it.

It was the University of Phoenix mission statement.

The "university" found nothing wrong with lifting—literally word for word except for the substitution of their institution's name—the educational mission of another institution.

A patently bogus postsecondary entity that made hundreds and hundreds of thousands of dollars selling degrees under color of California state authority for over ten years was denied licensure.

CHAPTER

17

Other Regulatory and Legislative Conflicts

Following the Arizona and California postsecondary licensure armistices, major political actions were mounted in response to the following:

- New Mexico Commission on Higher Education legislation to license University of Phoenix—because of its tax status—as a proprietary career school.
- Traditional academic standards for online education proposed by the Colorado Commission on Higher Education.

The diploma mill slur lost its political luster in capturing the attention of state legislators following scorched-earth political battles in Arizona and California, but other inspired methods of conflict emerged.

The State Higher Education Executive Officers Association monitored and coordinated postsecondary legislative and regulatory activities in all fifty states, and had New Mexico licensure of regionally accredited for-profit academic degree-granting institutions as career schools been enacted or traditional standards applied to computer-mediated learning in Colorado, it would have established precedents that could have very likely found their way into licensure laws of other states.

New Mexico Higher Education Range War

The New Mexico state university system—like Arizona's—failed to recognize higher education needs of working adults in a manner that allowed them constructive access to degree education. The University of Phoenix in Albuquerque and Santa Fe attracted hundreds of working adult students and enthusiastic business and industry support. New Mexico is in the North Central region, but the state universities refused to recognize University of Phoenix degrees and credits.

The state university system was embarrassed that the University of Phoenix met the higher education needs of New Mexico working adults. Rather than offer extended degree programs to meet that authentic need, they sought to end the embarrassment. This crass reaction had little or no impact on enrollment or educational support of New Mexico companies for their employees' attendance at the University of Phoenix.

The New Mexico Commission on Higher Education was faced with the abrupt closure of two career schools that left students with debt and no credentials, and introduced legislation to address the problem. The University of Phoenix was for profit, and though regionally accredited by the same entity that accredited New Mexico's colleges and universities, the commission demanded that it should meet proprietary career school licensure standards.

Political markings of the state university system were all over the proposal.

An accredited degree-granting institution serving seven hundred New Mexico working adults with eight hundred graduates—without one consumer complaint—we objected, solely because of our tax status, to being licensed as a career school.

The proposed licensing law, if passed, would affect the University of Phoenix in one deadly way: we would have to enter a "teach-out" agreement with another accredited New Mexico degree-granting institution. We filed annual Price-Waterhouse independently audited financial reports with North Central to enable them to discern if we were in danger because of financial exigency, something rarely, if ever, required of the type of mom n' pop career schools that chronically cease operation with no notice.

Career schools are usually mandated by state licensing statutes to have "teach-out" agreements with kindred schools because so many abruptly cease operation. Such agreements do not exist between accredited academic degree-granting institutions that recognize transfer of credits earned from individual course completion.

The only accredited private higher education institution in New Mexico offered liberal arts degrees to traditional-aged students, so the University of Phoenix would have to enter a "teach-out" arrangement with one of New Mexico's state universities.

The state university system's prior refusal to recognize University of Phoenix degrees or credits would have been used by the commission to deny licensure. If this precedent were established, other states would likely follow suit.

Due to the crush of budget legislation, the commission's bill failed to get to the senate floor prior to adjournment. The commission subsequently reintroduced identical legislation and the state university system pushed hard for its enactment. I hired a lobbying firm that successfully managed the passage of postsecondary education bonds. The lobbyist and I would meet at a coffee shop across the street from the state capitol to take the temperature of our political efforts. The director of the New Mexico State Financial Aid Board, a friend of the lobbyist, would usually join us.

On the day and at the same time the commission's legislation was being heard in the Senate Education Committee, we learned an identical bill was being heard in the House Education Committee. The bill died in the senate committee, but passed the house committee because no one was there to oppose it. I was advised subsequently that the director who'd joined our political meetings reportedly shared everything with lobbyists for the bill's passage. Despite the passage of legislation in the house identical to the legislation that failed in the senate, the commission bill never made it to the senate floor prior to *sine die*.

Following the legislative session, the director was charged with the alleged misuse of public funds and left office.

Cyber Diploma Mills in Colorado

In response to a prominent Colorado employer whose offices and plant were physically inaccessible from Denver during the winter, in the mid-1980s, University of Phoenix pioneered the use of an electronic blackboard linked to a computer for classes conducted through telephone conferencing. Snowbound working adult employees could attend conference call classes with instructors in Denver and sunny Phoenix. The company had repeatedly implored Colorado public universities to develop extended degree programs, but had received no cooperation.

The Colorado Commission on Higher Education proposed legislation to require out-of-state institutions providing electronic distance education—University of Phoenix then being only in- or out-of-state higher education institution to do so—to have electronically delivered programs evaluated and approved by the commission according to traditional capital-intensive academic standards.

Colorado recognized regional accreditation for licensure, and the proposal constituted an evaluation for accreditation using traditional standards appropriate for traditional-aged students at a single campus. Imposition of such requirements were unwarranted by consumer complaints or any evidence the University of Phoenix was providing electronically delivered education in any but a quality manner. Traditional standards would force the elimination of our highly innovative computer-mediated delivery system and prevent the employees of the Colorado company from earning their degrees.

Satisfied working adult students and their employer, along with our Colorado lobbyist, convinced the commission to abandon their proposal. If such legislation had passed, traditional standards would inevitably have been applied to the University of Phoenix on the ground operations in Colorado and set a dangerous regulatory precedent.

***

Why the University of Phoenix Survived

Given the wars, skirmishes, firefights, ambushes, dustups, attacks, melees, frays, brouhahas, rows, dry-gulching, bushwhacking, and sucker punching the University of Phoenix endured at the hands of traditional higher education, five factors ensured its survival and prosperity:

- High-quality educational content,
- Efficacy of the adult teaching/learning model,
- Candor, accuracy, and responsibility in all relationships,
- Political hard will to fight for survival on our merits, and
- Absolute accountability for student academic achievement.

If any of these factors had been faulty or frail, the University of Phoenix would be a footnote in the history and practice of higher education innovation in the twentieth and twenty-first centuries.

Pioneering efforts in the design of a teaching/learning model for working adults; curricular content and delivery; faculty training and quality control; academic quality management; assessment of learning outcomes; academic management and governance systems; administrative and financial systems; marketing, advertising, and student recruitment; computer-mediated learning; the provision of education to meet actual need; and the hard political defense of educational innovation and for-profit education can still lead the way in higher education in the new millennium.

CHAPTER

18

Home Front

John Sperling and I endeavored repeatedly to educate University of Phoenix managers of the centrality of politics in educational innovation, but I can't remember one who picked up the mantle or fully accepted its elemental role in the survival and evolution of a nontraditional higher education institution.

During the New Mexico academic range war, when I was occupied in California, a campus manager substituted for me at a meeting with the commission on higher education.

I met with the executive vice president and the manager to explain that regardless of any compromise proposed, no agreement must be made, because the bill would establish a dangerous national precedent. I checked in with the executive vice president on my return, and he reported the manager had gained valuable political experience. We called the manager and he proudly proclaimed that he had achieved a compromise on the bill.

The executive vice president and the manager believed they had done well by working cooperatively with the commission. They seemed to have little or no understanding of the regulatory precedent that would be established both in New Mexico and nationally with the passage of a bill that required the University of Phoenix to be licensed as a career school. Fortunately, due to the crush of budget legislation, the bill never made it to the floor of the senate prior to *sine die*.

Reaffirmations of Accreditation

I managed accreditation self-evaluations and was ordinarily the author and editor of self-studies provided to North Central's evaluation teams. One reaffirmation self-study was assigned to University of Phoenix's long-serving vice president for academic affairs. A month prior to the visit, I was given a draft copy. If submitted—in my opinion constructed so superficially—it could literally result in accreditation probation.

Evaluators unfamiliar with University of Phoenix's nontraditional teaching/learning model rely on the self-study for use in an on-site evaluation; if it lacks comprehensive and accurate description and documentation, it inevitably generates confusion rather than clarity. Confusion typically engenders a misapprehension of facts and stimulation of concerns, which if memorialized in the report of the visit—because it is part of a permanent evaluation record—develops a life of its own that could literally haunt the University of Phoenix in perpetuity.

I informed John Sperling of my opinion and, after reading the draft, he agreed that it had to be rewritten. The visit was scheduled in less than a month and request for postponement because the self-study wasn't completed would constitute evidence of lack of effective academic management.

A self-study helps improve the quality of an institution through the self-assessment of every aspect of its academic, operational, and financial structures and systems. A key element is involvement of all segments of the institution. A steering committee is established at the corporate level, and self-study committees formed at every campus and department to critically examine existing practices and procedures and recommend changes and improvements.

The process can consume a year.

Work products of committees are reviewed by the self-study steering committee and incorporated into the report. Committees were in the process of completing assessments, but the self-study draft did not reflect the benefit of the work product. John Sperling informed the academic vice president that I would be rewriting it.

For the next three and one half weeks I wrote fourteen hours a day, seven days a week. I completed the self-study section-by-section, and University of Phoenix's talented long-time graphic artist, Tom Bishop, laid the contents out for publication. There was so little time left before the visit that I was only able to circulate sections rather than the entire draft to faculty and staff. I completed the final draft, Bishop completed the layout for the printer, and the self-study was delivered to North Central on time.

Reaffirmation of Accreditation Visit

North Central always carefully observed conflict of interest rules in appointment of visiting teams, but the chair of this reaffirmation team possessed an unrevealed bias; he planned to open a Phoenix campus of his out-of-state institution to serve working adult learners. In the team report, he falsely accused Apollo Group of compromising the academic and institutional integrity of the University of Phoenix.

The University of Phoenix purchased corporate services from Apollo including financial management, purchasing, computer services, and facilities leasing. The stability of the holding company structure was elemental to the growth of the University of Phoenix and the plan to go public.

I prepared a detailed response documenting, among other things, that a super majority of University of Phoenix board members were public, some serving as long as eleven and no one less than three years. They were recognized in the community and many possessed experience in the operation of large organizations. No public member ever complained about a lack of independence when making decisions nor had experienced or known any interference from Apollo Group, nor did any faculty member ever complain about Apollo's interference with academic decision making.

The academic vice president said he would submit my response to the North Central committee charged with a review of the visit.

The academic vice president and I attended the review committee meeting. From the questions posed, the committee members had ignored my written response. The hole we were in only got deeper because the academic vice president failed to submit our response. I was relieved to come out of the review committee with a reaffirmation of accreditation for five years, with a focus visit in two.

I chaired the self-study steering committee for the next reaffirmation visit. Well in advance of the visit, I met with a new North Central liaison in Chicago. We reviewed progress University of Phoenix made in affirmatively addressing every concern identified by various evaluation teams over fifteen years, and I broached the idea of being granted a ten-year accreditation.

A common theme expressed by evaluation teams was that so many things were both changing and new at the University of Phoenix—we were perpetually improving academic policies and practices—that we should be kept on a five-year review leash to ensure that the changes actually worked. The liaison agreed that our track record was well established, and that as a mature institution, we might qualify for ten-year accreditation.

A little less than a year before the visit, I received a call from the liaison, his voice cold and distant. He asked about efforts to establish a campus in Hungary. The project had been going on forever under John Sperling, but remained developmental. "A representative of the University of Phoenix at a higher education conference in Budapest announced North Central approved degree programs in Hungary." No one had been authorized to make such a statement because it was simply not true.

The announcement apparently unleashed lurking suspicions in the mind of the new liaison.

Because of an accreditation announcement by someone operating under the authority of John Sperling, my credibility was seriously undermined with the new liaison. When I brought up the issue, John dismissed it as a bagatelle. Despite Sperling's lack of interest, I knew that the self-study for the upcoming visit had to be absolutely bulletproof.

Visit

From writing self-studies and managing accreditation visits, I knew that there was always at least one person—sometimes more—on each visiting team who prided him or herself on being assiduously confused about how the University of Phoenix functioned and managed itself academically. I had to describe the academic, operational, and financial aspects of the University of Phoenix so there was only one way to interpret them: precisely the way I wrote it.

Faculty and staff critically reviewed self-study iterations to ensure that descriptions and analyses of practices and procedures were consonant with how they actually functioned. When team members looked to see whether there were disparities between the way things were described and how they actually operated, they wouldn't find anything of consequence.

Reaffirmation of accreditation was essential to carry out the plan to go public within a couple of years.

The self-study was 608 pages long, perfect-bound, and heavy enough to keep a cow from flying away in a tornado. It was so comprehensively and accurately detailed that no matter how the evaluation team came at us, they couldn't get around it. I was glad I honored my instincts; the chair was out for bear.

A dean from a Jesuit university, the chair had a sinister scowl on his face and I knew we were in for serious problems when he asserted nastily and accusatorily that IPD had ghosted the self-study. Eight years following its humiliating loss to IPD, the chair of our reaffirmation of accreditation evaluation team apparently acquired the calumny from someone at fellow Jesuit Regis College.

Actually believing they didn't exist, he demanded to see the minutes of all the self-study committees, which I provided. Other documentation verifying all information contained in the self-study filled eight tables in the team meeting room.

One team member was North Central's learning-outcomes assessment expert. At that time, there was a push that institutions, independent of the faculty, assess the achievement of learning outcomes for each student. Unlike traditional institutions, the University of Phoenix expended significant staff and faculty time and money to develop and implement an academic quality-control system that included not only quality assessment by faculty and students, but the pre- and post-assessment of student knowledge and skills prior to and upon completion of the core curriculum leading to whatever degree they were earning.

Dr. Robert Tucker, a former member of the Phoenix faculty, was University of Phoenix's Senior Vice President of Research and Information Systems who developed and implemented a prodigious, cutting edge, metrics-rich academic-process management and learning outcomes assessment system. In addition to measuring incoming students' knowledge and capabilities, it provided a management tool to ensure that educational processes worked efficiently and effectively, that stated learning outcomes were achieved, and that desired professional impact in the workplace was in evidence.

Traditional colleges typically spent less than a dollar per student on "assessment," which meant they weren't doing learning outcomes assessment; we spent an estimated forty dollars.

Dr. Tucker wasn't interviewed until the third day of the visit, and from glancing into the visiting team meeting room prior to that important interview, the scowl on the face of the chair remained inviolate. Following the assessment expert's interview with Tucker and the examination of the assessment system and the university's application of the results, the next time I glanced into the room, the face of the team chair had been plowed into an expression of utter despondency.

University of Phoenix received a five-year reaffirmation of accreditation, the academic vice president subsequently resigned, I was appointed academic vice president, and two years later, Apollo Group went public.

I visited North Central headquarters to meet with their new executive director and a new liaison. I asked to see their file on the University of Phoenix. I expected, given the intensity and virulence of the public attacks by countless traditional academics over the previous fifteen years, to find an extensive record of complaints and explicit criticism. Moreover, I expected the file would contain documentation, no matter how fabricated, of alleged academic and financial malfeasance.

I found not one letter or any other type of correspondence from any student, staff member, faculty member, employer, legislator, news agency, or anyone from any public or private higher education system criticizing, condemning, complaining, or providing a scintilla of evidence of alleged academic malfeasance, or improper behavior on the part of anyone ever associated with the University of Phoenix, or the University of Phoenix itself.

Part Two

Mission Forsaken

Foreword

An argument can be made that as the result of becoming the largest accredited for-profit, publicly held private university in the nation—recognized as the gold standard in nontraditional higher education for working adults—the valuation of the stock of its holding company displaced its sole mission of providing education solely for working adults.

This was accomplished by the apparent sacrifice of its hard-earned status as the "gold standard" in nontraditional higher education for working adults in exchange for both a traditional and a non-traditional student demographic, some marginally employed, if at all, with high school diplomas and GEDs. Student census nearly tripled for a period of time and the price of Apollo stock reached its highest level in five years.

The elimination of historical admissions standards was a highly lucrative financial decision, but the educational impact of the open admissions policy remains inversely proportionate to the massive increase in Apollo Group's market capitalization and insider shareholder enrichment.

An offensive percentage of students admitted under the open admissions policy paid a heavy personal and financial price because so many were unable to realize gainful education. A large percentage of these students were academically and experientially unqualified to benefit from access to the learning they purchased. They dropped out unable to service student loan debt, and without degrees or meaningful employment.

The first responsibility of any professional is to do no harm. This elemental responsibility was apparently ignored for a substantial period of time following the IPO at the University of Phoenix and Apollo. An unwarranted price is being exacted from American taxpayers who foot the bill for the default of hundreds of millions of dollars in federal student loans for which these students became qualified solely from being admitted to the University of Phoenix.

CHAPTER

19

Beginning of the End and the End

I had a blind date with my future wife the day after her birthday. The following year, I informed John Sperling that I was considering my first marriage and he was oddly against it. When one is married, he reasoned, critical time otherwise spent in constructive endeavors must be dedicated to one's spouse if the marriage was going to succeed.

I didn't appreciate the personal consequences of failing to take his nuanced advice to heart.

In *Rebel With a Cause,* John Sperling's autobiographical book on the University of Phoenix and Apollo Group, he included a description of me—that predictably when I read it—I was happy to believe constituted a realistic account of my twenty-plus year history of work and friendship with him.

> *He was magnificent in a fight and I never would have succeeded in those battles without him. Whether we were writing endless self-studies and position papers explaining and justifying our system of education, making presentations before editorial boards and community organizations, or lobbying at the legislature, he was both effective and indefatigable. I suppose the source of much of our energy was the sheer joy of the fight. No one else had the energy to keep up with us, so we pretty much dominated the whole organization; we certainly determined strategy, tactics, and philosophy.*[91]

Later in *Rebel*, John took away what he had accorded me.

> *John withdrew from regular communication with me or any members of the management team. (H)e . . . charged me with forcing him out of the company.*[92]

I speculate that when John Sperling allowed me to buy a minority percentage of Apollo stock prior to the IPO, he believed it was a dowry for a lifetime marriage to that company. I was honored that John recognized my contributions in a material way and remain grateful. I abjectly failed to realize that my marriage constituted the end of my personal and professional relationship with John Sperling and the educational institution I helped create, nurture, and protect.

Unknown to me, John had hired a Washington, DC-based political operative, a former congressional staffer, to replace me. I had no knowledge of either the month of hiring or the meaning until I read *Rebel With a Cause* three years following my resignation. In *Rebel With a Cause,* John Sperling documented what the hiring meant:

> *(It) . . . ended any effective collaboration with Murphy.*[93]

Sperling characterized the hiring as a

> *(M)ajor change in our political operation . . . [that] . . . led to the departure of my comrade-in-arms, John Murphy.*[94]

John Sperling claimed he hired the new operative because

> *Murphy was unable to move from a regional to a national conception of the regulatory/political context in which Apollo operated.*[95]

The hiring of my replacement occurred the same month I got married.[96]

The following year, Sperling pointedly and strangely excluded me from negotiations with the U.S. Department of Education over the Carnegie Unit and its relationship to mandatory study groups. John later informed me—in an abruptly matter of fact manner—that a new political operative intervened successfully in this vital federal regulatory issue. When regulations were issued, there were no changes in the rules governing seat time. I pointed this out and John angrily ordered me to drop the subject.

The University of Phoenix and Apollo have subsequently paid hundreds of millions of dollars in fines and legal judgments because of violations of U.S. Department of Education regulations. A court ruled in 2011 that Apollo Group had to pay $145 million arising from a whistle-blower judgment. The United States Supreme Court had denied Apollo Group's appeal.

In *Rebel With A Cause,* John Sperling claimed he

> *(P)ressured a reluctant John Murphy to hire a Washington-based assistant . . . and for him to begin*

any analysis of the regulatory issues we would face in the states we had targeted for expansion. He resisted.[97]

Contrary to John's characterization, I completed a comprehensive state-by-state analysis of regulatory requirements and barriers, and made trips to Washington, DC to interview politically prominent law firms and lobbying groups. I recommended a well-known firm, but John rejected my recommendation out of hand because—unknown to me—he'd already hired someone else.

The pursuit of arguably cynical and transitory political fixes—instead of seeking and earning the academic and political validation that historically served University of Phoenix so effectively—has exacted an execrable financial and reputational price.

John's hiring of a new political operative unequivocally manifested his intention to end our two-decade-long personal, political, and intellectual collaboration. Over the next few years, he ordered me to resign as academic vice president, from membership on the California Council for Private Postsecondary Educational Institutions, and assigned the next self-study to someone else.

I believe he did so to force me out of the company.

Like so many other objectives John Sperling attained in his long life, he succeeded.

Going Public

At an Apollo Group executive retreat at the Ventana Hotel near Mt. Lemon in Tucson, Arizona, in the late 1980s, the decision was made to bring Apollo Group public. Once the IPO was subscribed to in the marketplace, the University of Phoenix would become the second publicly traded, nontraditional accredited for-profit higher education institution in the world.

The University of Phoenix won all its accreditation and political fights but remained a target of hostility in traditional higher education. We believed being vetted by investment bankers through the due diligence process—once the marketplace evidenced its affirmation of Apollo's (University of Phoenix's) academic universe through the purchase of stock—there were literally no more bona fides to be established.

A team from investment banks Smith-Barney and Alex. Brown held meetings at Apollo's law firm. Apollo's CFO was designated to represent the company in the construction of an IPO prospectus. Surprisingly—since Sperling had excluded me from all but formal executive meetings for a number of years—he asked that I represent Apollo. The CFO knew virtually nothing about our academic operations or educational philosophy. Presciently, I pondered whether it would be my last major contribution to the company.

Apollo IPO shares sold out and have increased thousands of percent.

Origins of the State of the Art Student Recruitment Machine

John Sperling retained a consultant from the business-management arm of Apollo's accountants, Price-Waterhouse, to optimize contemporary management practices at the University of Phoenix. Bill Gibbs, because of the contributions he made in accomplishing this vital task, was subsequently appointed president.

The University of Phoenix always had a strong marketing arm, but what it lacked when Bill Gibbs entered the picture was an effective sales arm. Gibbs orchestrated what arguably became the institutional raison d'être, student recruitment, for the University of Phoenix and Apollo. By 2010, Apollo and its subsidiaries employed some 8,000 recruiters.

Gibbs invested a reported $700,000 to bring student recruiters from all University of Phoenix's extended campuses to a sales and marketing meeting at the opulent Phoenician Hotel in the Arcadia neighborhood of Phoenix. The meeting inaugurated what turned out to be a wildly successful student recruitment apparatus.

Following Gibbs's departure after my resignation, the University of Phoenix and Apollo's overarching emphasis on student recruitment was formalized with the appointment of the former head of sales and marketing to run Apollo. Two former investment bankers later took over.

It was abundantly and humiliatingly clear that I could not make the contributions I had always been proud to make and I resigned. Fortunately, the increase in Apollo stock was such that I, and other "B" voting shareholding members who all departed within a couple years of my resignation—Bill Gibbs, Jerry Noble, President of the Institute for Professional Development, and Jim Hoggatt, Apollo Group Chief Financial Officer—were all financially independent.

School of Hard Knocks

There is a prized political lesson for anyone who works closely with the principal founder of a company. If supported personally and politically, you can accomplish remarkable things. Half or more of the work was away from the company, dealing with issues that most other executives only valued abstractly, so my company political base was tied exclusively to John Sperling. This relationship was critical because I dealt with forces that literally could put the University of Phoenix out of existence.

Failure was not an option.

Other principals and executives did not generally appreciate or enjoy political warfare, so their involvement would have resulted in unnecessary stress, confusion, and conflict. When political and personal support gets withdrawn, as John Sperling did the same month as my marriage by hiring someone to replace me, the consequences are personally painful and politically lethal within company ranks.

John Sperling hired someone to replace me on the sly, ordered me to resign prominent positions, deliberately excluded me from all but formal management meetings, and successfully doomed my status and place at both the University of Phoenix and Apollo Group.

From the moment John Sperling and I began to work together, he unfailingly backed my hand in dealing with both academic and political problems and issues. My reliance on John's steadfast support—not that we didn't engage perpetually in knock-down drag-out fights—not only allowed me to proceed confidently, but inspired answers to often insuperable-seeming problems.

John deliberately withdrew this support with the covert hiring of someone to replace me, and although I endeavored to constructively work through it for a number of years, it caused the end of both our professional and personal relationship.

I was stung by the dismissive, intermittently contemptuous manner in which I was treated over the years following my marriage prior to my forced resignation. I endeavored to work through it in honor of what John and I had been through, assuredly and opportunistically delayed by increases in Apollo stock valuation; but when it became painfully clear that I would be unable to continue to make material contributions to the organization I had always been proud to make, it was time to go.

What had happened to the improbable collaboration?

It appears that environment ultimately is, in fact, destiny.

I once asked John about his most poignant childhood memory. It occurred between the ages of seven and eight. For an entire year, he believed he was going to starve to death. My most poignant memories at that age were my tongue burned by molten Swanson's chicken pot pies in front of a grainy black-and-white television—along with headaches from mummifying loads of MSG and salt—and playing tennis with bald tennis balls.

I turned down continued funding when I perceived that my campus-community mental health program could no longer deliver the quality of services that had made a material difference in the lives of chronically mentally ill people, their families, the members of the neighborhood in which they lived, and the ordinary students who entered their lives. John Sperling, reviled for the disastrous professors' union walkout, risked his state university pension to fund a higher education consulting company, and mortgaged everything else to underwrite the creation and operation of the University of Phoenix.

We shared similar values.

The demise of the improbable collaboration commenced with my marriage and the surreptitious hiring of my replacement. Another material factor was the political and academic stabilization of the University of Phoenix.

We overcame every manner of academic and political challenge for almost twenty consecutive years and were institutionally positioned to entertain any new challenges because of 25 percent annual increases in enrollment. We were fast growing into an eight hundred pound nontraditional academic gorilla.

I was fast becoming expendable.

> *Inevitably, in a company that has had so many changes and has gone through so many stages of growth from start-up to maturity, every major repositioning of the Company has required a changing set of skills and attitudes. My job has to been to orchestrate this process by remaining emotionally aloof so that I can transfer, reassign, force out, or fire managers who have not grown with the company. I can then hire persons with the needed skills to replace them.*[98]

John Sperling hired someone to replace me the month I got married.

Apollo Group going public—along with the University of Phoenix—created the foundation for the displacement of the institutional goal that had defined every waking moment for nearly twenty-five years: building a higher education institution whose sole mission was meeting the higher educational needs of the working adult learner. The ultimate political and financial stabilization of that goal was attained through the establishment of a monetary valuation by bringing Apollo Group public.

Arguably, stock valuations eclipsed the founding mission. It resulted in the hiring of people—if measured by graduation and student loan default rates, regulatory fines, and legal judgments—with unrealized commitment to the optimum operation of an academic degree-granting institution solely for working adults.

They realized the immutable goal that appears to have displaced it; increased quarterly revenues and profits promoting and justifying increases in the valuation of Apollo Group stock, market capitalization, and executive salaries and bonuses. The University of Phoenix fought to keep itself free from the shackles of the traditional academic guild but subsequently appears to have shackled itself to the valuation of the publicly held stock guild.

Arguably, the pathology of increases in equity value displaced the values and absolute dedication to and protection of the integrity of the teaching/learning model by eliminating the three criteria that conditioned the efficacy of the teaching/learning model for working adults: age, current employment, and minimum work experience.

Never in my wildest imaginings did I contemplate that *The Butterball Effect* materialized repeatedly at private colleges IPD had saved from extinction, would manifest with me. Like IPD, once John Sperling deemed I was no longer useful, I had to go.

The once stellar academic achievements of the University of Phoenix in solely serving working adult learners have devolved—because of the elimination of admission requirements of age, employment, and experience—into marginal graduation rates and huge increases in student loan defaults. Add the payment of tens of millions of regulatory fines and hundreds of millions in lawsuits, and it appears to be the misanthropic cost of doing business.

Wither For-Profit Higher Education?

An operative question is whether any higher education institution should be structured on a for-profit economic construct, and even more importantly, whether it should be publicly traded given its inherent vulnerability to mission displacement because financial reward may trump academic integrity.

My answer—with major caveats—is yes.

If the University of Phoenix weren't structured as a profit-making enterprise with the fiscal discipline elemental to successful entrepreneurship, it wouldn't have survived. The for-profit corporate structure guaranteed the enmity of traditional higher education, but also ensured its longevity. The University of Phoenix pioneered an effective and highly successful teaching/learning model for adults, delivered in both physical and electronic venues, and contributed materially to the professional lives of its working adult students, society, and the economy.

The University of Phoenix teaching/learning model and delivery system needs to be replicated in every traditional higher education venue to meet the needs of America's nontraditional undergraduate student population.

Evolution into a Public Trust

The issue of goal replacement resulting in the forsaking of a founding mission in favor of increasing market capital and stock valuation can be addressed through the mandate that accrediting agencies enforce their substantive change guidelines and, at a certain point in time, ownership transitions to a public trust, much like pharmaceutical products that become generic once risk takers realize a return on their investment. Another option to facilitate the development of such needed enterprises is to attach them to traditional academic degree-granting institutions, where, at some future point in time, the profits from the enterprise become an endowment.

The overarching standard in the operation of all for-profit educational institutions is that they be materially accountable for the educational achievements of their students. Being structured as profit making brings with it such pristine accountability.

* * *

The University of Phoenix was an exhilarating, terrifying, preposterous, painful, and extraordinary ride, and three quarters of the time was the most fun I ever have had in my life. Everything runs its course, however, particularly when success is accompanied by an abundance of financial reward.

When a dream is achieved, you find a new one.

CHAPTER

20

Educational Mission

The University of Phoenix was granted accreditation and its nontraditional teaching/learning model for working adults became recognized as an academically legitimate method of providing academic degree programs. Key to that recognition was that learning outcomes equivalent to those delivered according to the Carnegie Unit seat-time/learning equation could be delivered successfully via a teaching/learning construct designed specifically for the working adult learner.

In its unified form, the teaching/learning model had been determined, after serial evaluations for over two decades, to be achieving the purposes for which it had been designed. To function properly and effectively, students admitted into bachelor's programs were required to be at least twenty-three years of age, and be employed at the time of admission with a minimum of two years of work experience.

During my tenure at the University of Phoenix, virtually every one of its critical problems arose because of intractable external opposition by traditional academics and their political allies and minions. Opposition was driven by philosophical and moral objection to higher education being provided for profit, and based on that objection, condemnation—as fundamentally corrupt and generically inferior—of innovation that differed from the traditional way of doing things, allegedly because it is designed solely to maximize profits.

Confronted at its founding by what proved to be enduring hostility and criticism, the University of Phoenix was transparent in all its activities, not the least being that it was the subject of ongoing regulatory examinations, including by the IRS. Living in a glass bunker, we had to be absolutely forthright in how we described and explained ourselves. We could never claim anything as fact without ensuring that it was precisely correct.

We were never accorded a margin of error.

During those politically and financially tumultuous years, we were never fined or sanctioned by any state or federal regulatory agency, nor did we pay judgments arising from whistleblower and other lawsuits. Our graduation rate exceeded traditional tax-supported and equaled nonprofit private colleges and universities.

Since 1999 when the University of Phoenix was fined by the U.S. Department of Education for allegedly violating loan repayment and reimbursement regulations,[99] virtually all its educational, regulatory, and legal problems appear to have originated, not solely from external sources as in its first twenty-five years, but from internal management decisions and practices.

The original teaching/learning model remains viable for working adult students for whom it was designed, but it does not—evidenced by marginal graduation rates and spikes in student loan defaults—appear to be educationally viable for younger, inexperienced, and perhaps unemployed or marginally employed students whose sole qualification for enrollment is a high school diploma or GED.

What the University of Phoenix did to itself is similar to what occurred in the investment banking industry when it plunged into the subprime mortgage market. Once only qualified borrowers were granted loans commensurate with their economic history and ability to pay; then over a short period of time, millions of homebuyers economically unqualified to assume mortgages became qualified recipients. The result was the cratering of real estate and the economy.

Since 2004, the University of Phoenix's open admissions policy allowed virtually any eighteen-year-old with a high school diploma or GED to enroll.

It's like starting a seventy-pound ten-year-old Pop Warner football player as a NFL interior lineman.

Open-ended admissions resulted in the enrollment of students with little or no meaningful work experience—including current employment—into its degree programs. Like homeowners unqualified to pay mortgages undeservedly received, they were often incapable of realizing gainful education derived from a proven teaching/learning model solely for working adults.

Unfortunately, a high percentage of these individuals were and are academically and experientially unprepared to take advantage of education provided by the University of Phoenix. They not only fail to graduate, but are burdened with the repayment of loans that will dog many for a lifetime.

The financial value extracted through the sale of Apollo stock appears to have an inverse relationship to the achievement of what were once stellar qualities at the University of Phoenix; high graduation and low student loan default rates, and absolute accountability for educational quality, practices, and outcomes minimally expected from a for-profit higher education institution.

In its infancy and continuing for a period of time after Apollo Group went public, the University of Phoenix prided itself—because it was for-profit—on being accountable for the quality of everything done in its name. The same could not be said for tax-supported institutions.

The root cause of regulatory and whistleblower scandals arising from management decisions at the University of Phoenix is linked in part to the forsaking of the University of Phoenix's founding mission and purposes. The open admissions policy cast off this founding educational focus and delimited it so the University of Phoenix now serves the same students as traditional higher education institutions, but without the requisite capital-intensive support system.

Apollo Group created two-year Axia College to meet the legitimate educational needs of noncollege-educated, inexperienced, nontraditional and traditional-aged students who failed to meet historical University of Phoenix admissions standards.

Apollo Group was extensively and painfully experienced with problems inherent in educating persons with high school diplomas and GED certificates. Apollo purchased a vocational/technical school in Las Vegas and a keyboarding school in Phoenix. Christened Alta Tech, career schools were added in California, Nevada, and Texas. Alta Tech relentlessly lost money, some $3.3 million over three years alone. Alta Tech was sold prior to Apollo Group's IPO.

Making Axia College part of the University of Phoenix inaugurated a supercharged student recruitment juggernaut that, at one point, almost tripled University of Phoenix enrollment. Relentless focus on student recruitment gave rise to chronic educational failures that cost American taxpayers millions of dollars.[100]

University of Phoenix Mission and Purposes

A higher education institution's mission and purposes—traditional and nontraditional—inform all aspects of its academic and financial operations. The evaluation to the extent to which it achieves its mission and purposes is elemental in the evaluation for accreditation or reaffirmation of accreditation.

It is the fulcrum on which an institution balances itself in the achievement of its educational goals and objectives.

The University of Phoenix absolutely possessed the right to modify its mission and purposes to broaden service to traditional-aged students. Concomitant with such a right—including the absolute right to sell Apollo stock in the open market—was the requirement for the massive restructuring of its academic delivery system to recognize and accommodate the learning needs and abilities of a traditional-student demographic.

Such restructuring affects the entire academic operation and is something that can only occur over time.

It appears that the University of Phoenix enrolled hundreds of thousands of students under the open admissions policy during the time it was engaged in the lengthy and exceedingly complex process of effecting this arterial educational change. It did so because of the apparent default of the Higher Learning Commission of North Central that allowed the change in mission and student body to occur without a publicly documented substantive change evaluation.

The original mission and purposes statement was the foundation for the development, implementation, and refinement of its teaching/learning model for working adult students. For more than two decades it served as the touchstone for every aspect of its operation as an academic degree-granting higher education institution. Despite its clarity and unambiguous focus, it required years to institutionalize properly.

When two-year Axia College was made part of the University of Phoenix it was like chaining a massive oceangoing barge brimming with federally guaranteed student loan money to the tail of an F-18 fighter jet. The federally guaranteed student loan money has been off-loaded, but neither the barge nor the jet appears to have moved a millimeter.

A higher education institution's mission and purposes inform each discrete aspect of its academic and financial operation. If those aspects are not modified commensurate with changes in mission and purposes, there will be a major disconnection between what the institution purports to be doing and what it is actually doing.

The University of Phoenix was once dedicated solely to the provision of education to working adults and all its operating rules and procedures properly reflected that educational focus. Upon the loss of that focus through the change in its founding mission, the University of Phoenix joined the ranks of thousands of other traditional higher education institutions, but without the requisite academic management and student support system. The results speak for themselves.

Part Three

Gainful Education

Gainful Education

For-Profit Education

The for-profit sector became a major player in twenty-first century postsecondary education largely for the following reasons:

- Traditional nonprofit and public postsecondary education is designed and operated to serve eighteen-to-twenty-four-year-olds at single campuses primarily during the day between September and May, and often fails to meet the educational needs of the "New American majority"[101] nontraditional students who now make up two-thirds of all undergraduate students;
- The University of Phoenix pioneered innovative, cost-effective, non-capital-intensive, accreditable, and replicable classroom-based and online degree education delivery systems that attracted private equity in the open market;

- Apollo Group's (APOL)—the University of Phoenix holding company—stock appreciated thousands of percent since its sold-out initial public offering in the mid-1990s;
- U.S. taxpayers underwrite up to 100 percent of the for-profit sector's revenue through federally guaranteed student loans, grants, and other public educational benefits; and
- Wall Street vetted for-profit postsecondary education as a growth industry.

For-Profit Political Presence

Thirty of the largest for-profit postsecondary institutions that enroll 75 percent of the students in this sector are operated and managed by well-educated, politically sophisticated, and exceedingly well-compensated corporate and financial executives often adroit at interpreting laws and regulations devised, interpreted, and enforced by civil servants and volunteer accreditation evaluators.

Like their kindred spirits in the corporate world, they craft intelligent and imaginative ways to minimize regulatory reach, influence, and interference. Laws and regulations that are conflicting, ambiguous, poorly defined, or queasily interpreted—not uncommon to educational regulation—are nimbly countered to protect the operational and financial interests of the enterprise.

Many at for-profit postsecondary institutions don't believe they have responsibility to decrypt education statutes and regulations, particularly when they remain the subject of endless reinterpretation and revision. This corporate value leaves many in traditional postsecondary education aghast, but it is the way modern businesses deal with sometimes impenetrable, often conflicting laws and regulations, especially from competing bureaucracies.

The U.S. Department of Education is responsible for developing regulations based on its interpretation of laws governing the primary revenue source for for-profit postsecondary institutions—federally guaranteed student loans—and being a governmental entity, is highly disposed to political influence. Between January 2010 and October 2011, the largest for-profit postsecondary institutions and allied trade groups invested the following in political lobbying:[102]

Washington Post Company (Kaplan)	$1.7 million
Coalition for Educational Success	$1.7 million
Career Education Corporation	$1.6 million
Association of Private Sector Colleges and Universities	$1.5 million
Apollo Group	$1.4 million
Corinthian College	$1.4 million
Education Management Corporation	$1.4 million
Bridgepoint Education	$1.2 million
TOTAL	**$11.9 million**

In 2010, the for-profit higher education sector employed 158 lobbyists.

The political influence of the for-profit sector is now formidable in the construction, interpretation, and application of higher education policy and regulation, as well as persuading Congress to acknowledge and enact their will. The for-profit sector applies the same political horsepower and skill with state regulators and accreditation entities.

Twenty-first-century for-profit postsecondary education drives a turbo-charged, nitro-powered formula racecar equipped with cutting edge political horsepower. Federal, state, and accreditation regulators crouch on an early twentieth century ox-drawn bureaucratic wagon mired in a well-financed lobbying bog.

What's at Stake

Millions of dollars in private equity are invested annually in private for-profit higher education, but even these substantial amounts are vastly overshadowed by the ongoing investment by American taxpayers in all postsecondary education. In 2003, taxpayer-funded federal student loan debt totaled $253 billion; in 2012, it was $966 billion.[103]

In 2010—11, American taxpayers invested $32 billion[104] in federal loans and grants in for-profit postsecondary education. This sector now consumes 25 percent of U.S. Department of Education student loans.[105] Students in the for-profit sector represent 13 percent of all postsecondary students, but 47 percent of the loan defaults.[106]

The for-profit sector commonly justifies profit by making a virtue of providing education to nontraditional students—many high risk and minority—who are underserved or not served by traditional higher education. The sector asserts that high dropout and student loan-default rates are endemic to its student demographic.

Even if these percentages did arise solely from student demographics, it does not obviate sector responsibility for poor academic persistence and excessive student loan default rates.

The ever-increasing need for postsecondary education, reduction in financial support at public institutions, continuing increases in percentages of nontraditional students, and annual increases in costs of undergraduate education at traditional postsecondary institutions at nearly five times the rate of inflation since 1978,[107] makes the role of private enterprise in postsecondary education—despite its sometimes obdurate financial profile—essential to the economic and social health of the nation.

The for-profit sector is commonly disparaged by higher education traditionalists and some members of congress for its over dependence on federal and state tax dollars for revenue, and—despite American taxpayer investment of tens of billions of dollars in federally guaranteed loans and grants over the last twenty years—the failure to educate an unacceptably high percentage of its students.

The for-profits are not the only sector of postsecondary education in which an unacceptably high percentage of its students fail to attain their educational goals.

Traditional Sector

The traditional public postsecondary sector receives substantially greater taxpayer benefits than the for-profit sector and exhibits failure largely without public opprobrium; only 57 percent of full-time students graduate after six years. The six-year graduation rate is 45 percent for low-income students, 39 percent for African Americans, and 27 percent for students over 25 years of age.[108]

Despite its flaws and what seems like unflagging criticism, the for-profit sector is often innovative, has a prejudice for action, and is a leader in the delivery of nontraditional postsecondary education in the digital age. If traditional higher education manifested similar behaviors, higher education, society, and the economy could realize huge benefits.

The academic architecture of traditional postsecondary education, institutionalized in the late 19th century, often fails to serve nontraditional students effectively, and has a shared governance structure—administration and faculty—that intractably frustrates substantive and timely innovation and change. Private enterprise can prove to be—coupled with a "gainful education" regulatory standard (See p. 233) integrated into the current regulatory triad applicable to for-profit, nonprofit, and public institutions alike—a cost-effective and accountable source of high-quality postsecondary education.

The key to the optimum functioning of all postsecondary education is the recognition and acceptance that all profit-making, nonprofit, and public institutions must be explicitly accountable for the educational performance of their students.

American taxpayers face a difficult time continuing the open-ended support of postsecondary education during a period of dangerously high deficits, an economic system seemingly unable to operate at full capacity, sustained economic erosion of the middle class, unacceptable primary, secondary, and postsecondary educational outcomes, relentless increases in the cost of a college degree, and towering student loan debt.

Traditional Higher Education

Traditional college tuition and fees increased 1,120 percent between 1978 and 2012.[109] This eye-popping, jaw-dropping, head-spinning rise in the cost of traditional postsecondary education heartlessly shames the increases in other major sectors of the American economic and social structure:

- Health Care: 600 percent,
- Shelter: 300 percent,
- Consumer Price Index (CPI), 200 percent, and
- Food: 200 percent.

If sea changes to the fundamental concepts that circumscribe the manner in which the American postsecondary education functions—for-profit, nonprofit, and public alike—are not made immediately, it risks becoming an academic, financial, and political calamity that will permanently demoralize America's belief and investment in the transformative power of postsecondary education.

If this is allowed to happen, the public and private postsecondary education system—as we know and understand it—will irretrievably collapse, and very likely with it, the future of our nation. These grave challenges to postsecondary education must be placed in the context of the other challenges we collectively face.

Systemic Challenges

Baby Boomer Retirement

By 2030, 78 million baby boomers will have retired and virtually all will receive Social Security and Medicare benefits. Life expectancy continues to lengthen, as will the years required to underwrite these benefits. Medicare costs spike annually at multiples of the inflation rate and, and without substantive reform, are indisputably unaffordable without a material increase in the number of people active in the workforce in relationship to those no longer active.

Unfunded Civil Service Pensions and Benefits

Over the last four decades, state and local governments seeded the growth of public service pensions and benefits by substituting unfunded increases in retirement benefits for those in salaries and wages. Serial decision making with consequences manifested in the future has morphed into a rapacious beast poised to devour the public's largesse in both a marginally performing economy and a politically polarized nation.

Unfunded and underfunded public service pensions and benefits have been estimated to reach some $3 trillion together with a decline in tax revenues and an aging electorate.

Cost Increases in Traditional Higher Education

Over the last three decades, the costs of traditional higher education have risen annually at nearly five times the rate of inflation. To compensate for these staggering increases—instead of developing innovative, cost-effective, high-quality alternatives in response to changing student demographics and societal needs—the amount of money students are allowed and encouraged to borrow is relentlessly increased.

It is widely recognized that increases in federal loans and grants are usually matched by increases in tuition and other costs in both the for-profit and not-for-profit postsecondary sectors.

In 2013, the average traditional college graduate reportedly carries some $25,000—not counting parental loans and credit cards—in educational debt that cannot be discharged except in rare circumstances. Educational debts now dog holders for a lifetime. Any American receiving

Social Security benefits who possesses federal student loan debt—whether personally or on behalf of someone else—will have payments subtracted from their Social Security stipends until the debt is satisfied.

Investment in America's Infrastructure

The physical infrastructure that facilitates and promotes development, production, and growth—highways, streets, bridges, levees, ports, public schools, electrical grids, water systems, waste systems, and public transportation services—has steadily deteriorated because of myopic decision making, taxpayer resistance, and political leadership. Infrastructure repair, replacement, improvement, and expansion are estimated to cost between $3 and $4 trillion. To maintain America's leadership in a global economy—with concomitant economic, political, and military power—we unconditionally must make this investment sooner rather than later.

Consumer Debt

Consumer debt dipped slightly with the collapse of the economy in 2008, but American consumers owe a reported $11 trillion due to often permissive and sometimes predatory credit policies that allowed tens of millions of us to live beyond our means.

National Security and Ability to Compete in a Global Economy

Today, 75 percent of the applicants to the U.S. armed services are rejected because of their failure to pass aptitude tests and physicals, and/or possessing criminal records.[110] This phenomenon carries over to the private sector where job applicants—high school and college graduates—often fail to possess the basic knowledge and skills to succeed in a global, highly sophisticated twenty-first century, digital-age workplace.

Lack of Corporate Faith in America

Belief in the future of the United States, evidenced by investment in the economy, suffers from an indecent lack of commitment and politicized risk aversion by some corporate leaders. Young adults posit their hope and faith in their country through the assumption of increasingly risky educational debts, and taxpayers dutifully underwrite public and private higher education because of their unwavering commitment to the continued economic, social, and political health of the nation.

Corporate America sits on an estimated $3 trillion—about half held offshore to avoid taxes—that should be invested responsibly in the nation that provides them the foundation for their success.

Prominent corporate leaders pule about government regulation and lack of consumer demand, but maintain their exalted position in the economic status quo—minimizing risk and maximizing profits and executive bonuses—by restricting increases in employee compensation, not hiring, and failing to create businesses that operate physically in the United States. Such conduct does not honor or exemplify the values and beliefs on which this nation was built and evidences a startling dissonance with the economic patriotism of the vast majority of Americans.

Most galling, such craven behavior repudiates the core values of our nation.

More of the Same

In virtually every economic sector of American society, innovation and change are elemental to continued success. American companies struggle to improve efficiency, produce more with less, and create new products and services that meet the needs of both the domestic and global marketplace.

Traditional postsecondary education products are still fundamentally the same as they have always been—with new disciplines and concentrations presaging and acknowledging advancements in the workplace, research, and scholarship—but because traditional colleges and universities are capital intensive, the cost of providing essentially the same products year after year costs excessively more.

There is no expectation these costs will level off, and the price of a traditional college degree ruthlessly outpaces the public's ability to pay for it. Traditional postsecondary education is at an economic crossroads; if its capital-intensive method of operation is not modified, an ever-increasing number of people will be prevented from attending because of the cost, and that caustic reality is already eroding America's optimism about and belief in higher education.

These looming threats to the economic, social, and political order provide the opportunity to accomplish changes that otherwise would be angrily and resentfully condemned and dismissed. One major change must occur in the postsecondary regulatory apparatus, the "triad."

Postsecondary Regulatory Triad

The July 2012 report of the Senate Health, Education, Labor and Pension (HELP) Committee—*For Profit Higher*

Education: The Failure to Safeguard the Federal Investment and Ensure Student Success concluded that the regulatory triad of federal, state, and accreditation agencies is structurally and operationally incapable—without substantive reform—of effectively regulating the for-profit sector.

The for-profit education sector is often at philosophical and fiduciary odds with the traditional higher education and the regulatory triad that oversees it: U.S. Department of Education, state-licensing agencies, and private nongovernmental accrediting associations. The triad was originally designed to regulate traditional nonprofit and public institutions that deliver education primarily on campuses, during the day, to eighteen-to-twenty-four-year-olds, between September and May.

The for-profit postsecondary sector delivers education twenty-four hours a day, seven days a week, three hundred sixty-five days a year to virtually anyone over eighteen years-of-age.

The regulatory triad remains flummoxed. The principal impediment to substantive reform is the structure of the triad itself. Each leg has its own mission, regulatory architecture, philosophical values, and political influences. The problem is exacerbated by two legs being governmental and one nongovernmental.

The for-profit sector is well financed, politically sophisticated, and committed to, experienced, and adept in protecting and advancing its monolithic financial interests.

The federal leg, the U.S. Department of Education, is part of the executive branch but is susceptible to legislative-branch political influence. The state leg is beholden to the executive and legislative branches and to the institutions they license. Federal and state agencies are subject to intervention by the judicial branch. Because of the separation clause of the U.S. Constitution, states usually prevent or minimize federal interference in the regulation of postsecondary education.

The third leg, accrediting associations, are regional and national private nongovernmental voluntary associations that operate on the fees and dues paid by the institutions they accredit, and integrate representatives of their accredited institutions into their governance and evaluation structure.

Participation is voluntary on the part of those who conduct accreditation evaluations and occupy their boards, panels, commissions, and accreditation teams, as is accreditation itself. They are rarely, if ever, subject to federal, state, or even judicial intervention, much less governmental monitoring or control.

Accrediting agencies strive to improve and maintain educational quality through voluntary peer review. They are not consumer-protection agencies, but evaluate institutions in light of their individually defined educational missions and purposes to promote institutional improvement. It is common for accreditation to be granted for periods of five to ten years. Ordinarily, in the absence of substantive change, financial exigency, moral improbity, or change in control or ownership, institutions are usually left to their own devices for the entire term.

These yawning evaluation windows are eminently suited to traditional postsecondary education where the pace of innovation and change—other than sometimes availing itself of cutting-edge nomenclature to doll-up hidebound practices—is geologic. It is manifestly unsuitable for effectively regulating the fast-moving and politically sophisticated for-profit postsecondary education sector.

Regulatory schemes predicated on multiple, independent, and inherently dissonant bureaucracies to address chronic problems with for-profit postsecondary education simply does not and will not work. Given the investment by the for-profit sector in its state of the art political lobbying apparatus, it's highly unlikely to materialize in any substantive manner. The simpler, more democratic, and minimally bureaucratized the solution, the better the chance of success.

Because of the cratering of the economy in 2008, many states eliminated or curtailed postsecondary education licensure activities with private for-profit institutions, defaulting to the U.S. Department of Education and accrediting agencies for quality control and consumer protection.

The federal department of education and accrediting associations are not structured to assume these important responsibilities. Many states still provide some consumer protection, but when the numbers of students are as vast as those enrolled in for-profit institutions—more than half who may attend online—timely and meaningful protection is marginal at best.

Century-Old Regulatory Model

The regulatory triad came into being when postsecondary education was circumscribed by physical location, religiously observed a 1906 Carnegie Unit pedagogic model, and operated on a late-nineteenth-century agrarian calendar.

Two reasons for the regulatory triad's shortcomings are that many for-profit institutions have multiple physical operations in a multitude of states, and education is commonly delivered online independent of geographical regulatory tracking. Another is that for-profit institutions are managed as businesses, so when an opportunity presents itself and makes business sense—unlike at most traditional higher education institutions—action is often quickly taken.

Some for-profit institutions appear in constant flux, a cardinal sin in traditional postsecondary education. Many institutions—particularly those offering online education—don't conform to the late-nineteenth-century agrarian-calendar-based September-to-May academic year, students start educational programs every month of the year.

The triad's traditional measures for tracking and measuring student progress often no longer apply.

The postsecondary education regulatory triad was designed and is operated in acknowledgement of the geologic pace of change at traditional colleges and universities. Applied to the digital-age operations of for-profit institutions in a global economy, it leaves federal, state, and accreditation regulators often slogging through the statutory outback with a bureaucratic witching stick trying to divine what to do.

Reimagining and Reinventing the Triad

The inherent ability of governmental and nongovernmental bureaucracies to either impede or restrain the organizational alacrity and reach of the for-profit postsecondary sector is negligible. The triad that helps ensure quality in traditional nonprofit, public, and for-profit postsecondary education must be *re*imagined, *re*invented, and *re*institutionalized if it is going to play a meaningful role in the provision of higher education in the twenty-first century, particularly in ensuring that private enterprise continues to play its elemental function in the delivery of postsecondary education for millions of nontraditional students.

Traditional postsecondary institutions alone cannot and will not meet this nation's compelling educational needs.

Baseline Literacy and Numeracy

Applicants to traditional public and private academic degree-granting higher education institutions and vocational/technical/career schools must be required to pass a baseline literacy and numeracy test. Accompanying this policy is the requirement that no accredited higher education institution or postsecondary vocational/technical/career school can receive or use any tax dollars—including state and federal student loans and grants—in the provision of remediation to any student subsequent to admission.

Evidenced by dropout rates at academic degree-granting institutions and career schools, an unacceptable percentage of students do not possess the intellectual foundation and knowledge base for gainful education. Those who drop out are often burdened with crushing student loan debt and no change or even diminishment of employability.

An estimated 20 percent of students—some 4 million—admitted to traditional colleges and universities lack baseline literacy and numeracy. Tax dollars appropriated for the provision of higher learning must be spent on remediation to ensure that those already admitted are capable of gainful education. This forces taxpayers to pay again for education provided at the primary and secondary school level, prolongs the completion of degree requirements and entrance into the workforce, and violently increases the cost of earning a degree.

Career schools—the University of Phoenix and some public community colleges—generate the highest student loan default rates because they grant admission to virtually any eighteen-year-old with a high school diploma or GED. To enforce the requirement that all persons admitted to postsecondary institutions evidence the intellectual capability for gainful education, admission to an accredited postsecondary institution must no longer automatically qualify anyone for a federal or state loan or grant.

There are a glut of idiosyncratic reasons for the failure rates at traditional colleges and universities: students unqualified to realize gainful education; students dropping in and out at will; and forcing full-time working adults over twenty-five—who compose more than half of the college-going population—to earn degrees in a physically centralized learning system designed for eighteen-to-twenty-four-year-olds operating on a late-nineteenth century agrarian calendar.

Gainful Education Standard

A fair and comprehensive way to regulate all players in the education-industrial complex—including the traditional nonprofit and public sector—is the institution of a gainful education standard as the gatekeeping mechanism for all governmental loans and grants:

> *Applicants to accredited postsecondary education institutions shall pass a baseline examination evidencing their intellectual capacity and knowledge base to benefit gainfully from education underwritten by American taxpayers.*

The adoption of the gainful education standard can

- Minimize illiterate people from being wrongly targeted for postsecondary educational recruitment,
- Eliminate qualification for governmental loans and grants solely by admission to an accredited postsecondary institution,
- Materially increase graduation rates,
- Significantly reduce federal student-loan default rates,
- Transform the quality and performance of the American workforce,
- Encourage the creation and expansion of American business and industry on American soil employing American workers,
- Establish a foundation for the growth of the economy and the resurrection of the middle class,
- End primary and secondary school social promotion to provide the operative basis for the reform of the public K-12 system, and
- Stabilize and protect the role and place of for-profit postsecondary education.

Benefits of the Gainful Education Standard

Ensuring that individuals admitted to accredited postsecondary institutions possess the intellectual foundation and knowledge base to benefit gainfully from any tax-supported educational endeavor will not only result in the massive cost savings needed to address American's deficit, but ultimately transform K-12 education because no one who is not literate or numerate will receive public postsecondary education benefits.

The gainful education standard ends pernicious social promotion and provides the political and practical foundation for substantive K-12 reform. As long as students are admitted to postsecondary educational institutions who are incapable of gainful education, K-12 education will never be reformed.

The gainful education standard minimizes the need for multiple—and ultimately toothless—regulatory bureaucracies to ensure educational quality and outcomes, because most students will possess intellectual and emotional self-esteem to exercise their role as critical consumers of educational products and services; very much like University of Phoenix's working adult students once served successfully in the context of its founding mission.

The promise of the gainful education standard will generate a cataclysm of opposition and dire predictions of economic and social perdition, particularly when accompanied by the prohibition that no tax dollars can be expended in the provision of remediation for anyone admitted to an accredited postsecondary institution. Once things have settled down, a new educational sector will emerge to meet the compelling national need for our citizens to become literate and numerate.

It's the American Way.

Systemic Reform in Traditional Higher Education

There are a number of fundamental reforms that can be enacted immediately to reduce the costs and improve efficacy of traditional higher education while preserving its vital role in the society and the economy.

Adults Over Twenty-Five

Students twenty-five and older completing the requirements for associate's and bachelor's degrees must attend off-campus and/or online degree programs. These adults—virtually all who work—do not require a geographically bound, capital-intensive learning environment structured and managed to meet the learning and social needs of eighteen-to-twenty-four-year-olds.

Working adult students can be served in a more cost- and time-efficient, educationally productive manner, complementing their workplace responsibilities through the completion of degree requirements at satellite campuses and online courses. Tax-supported colleges and universities must offer rolling enrollments where working adult students can begin degree programs any month of the year, once a minimum number of other working adults join a virtual learning group. Working adult students complete course requirements sequentially—one accelerated course at a time—until degree requirements are satisfied.

Courses Required to Complete Degrees

All accredited public and private colleges and universities must guarantee courses required to earn a degree are available for completion within the time specified to earn that degree. No student should ever be forced to delay graduation due to the unavailability of any course.

Transfer Credit Acceptance

All academic credits earned at regionally accredited public and private colleges and universities must be accepted toward the satisfaction of degree requirements at other accredited institutions. Virtually every individual employed professionally at an accredited college or university possesses a degree—including advanced and terminal degrees—from an accredited college or university.

An unacceptable percentage of students who bring credits earned from like institutions have those credits denied for transfer and are forced to pay for and retake courses. Redundant learning is needlessly time-consuming and unacceptably costly because it lengthens both the completion of degree requirements and entrance into the workplace.

Full-Time Attendance

Full-time attendance for eligibility of federal and state financial aid at academic degree-granting institutions must be defined as fifteen per semester—or equivalent quarter—units. Until the 1970s, a full-time credit load was fifteen credit hours. Since then, it has been twelve hours—even as low as nine—and the exceedingly costly result is the lengthening of the time to earn a degree. This policy is financially beneficial to institutions because it keeps students in the tuition pipeline, but is economically disastrous because annual increases in attendance costs continue to outpace inflation, and completion of degree requirements is unacceptably prolonged.

Faculty Teaching Load

Full-time faculty, many of whom carry marginal teaching loads of three, six, and nine credit hours, must be required to carry a standard twelve-credit load. The reduction in teaching load while receiving full salaries results in increased cost of earning a degree because adjunct faculty and/or graduate students must be hired to make up the difference.

Maximum Eligibility Period for Tax-Supported Postsecondary Education

One way to immediately increase the ratio of those working to those not working while lowering higher education expenditures and debt, is to establish the maximum number of years individuals are eligible—qualified for gainful education—to have the cost of their education underwritten by taxpayers. Individuals must remain eligible to earn an associate's degree underwritten by taxpayers for a maximum of two contiguous years, and a bachelor's degree for four contiguous years. If an individual fails to earn a degree within these parameters, the actual cost of that education is entirely their financial responsibility.

American postsecondary education culture is one where individuals can earn credentials at their own pace because they are permitted to drop in or out at will. The financial burden of such an endlessly forgiving educational system is now economically unsustainable. Millions of young people remain lost to the workforce into their middle to late twenties with an accompanying delay in maturation and acceptance of the responsibilities of adulthood. We can no longer afford to support an educational system in which the average time-to-degree at public higher education institutions is six years for the 57 percent who actually graduate, particularly when the percentage of the population active in the work force will diminish to economically unsustainable levels.

K-12 System Reform

Public primary and secondary schools were designed and operated to ensure that graduates were literate and numerate. Distressingly, hundreds of thousands of students drop out annually, and an embarrassing percentage of those who do graduate are not capable of gainful education at the postsecondary level. High school dropouts are largely illiterate and doomed to suffer the social and economic consequences of that intellectual status for a lifetime.

Adult illiteracy in the United States now represents about 20 percent of our population, some 60 million people.

Sincere and expensive efforts have been undertaken over the last thirty years to raise academic achievement levels of public primary and secondary students, but there have only been marginal increases in reading comprehension and mathematics scores. An individual student's academic success or failure was once the student's responsibility. This changed when test scores were aggregated as the measure of achievement.

Test aggregation shifted the accountability from the individual student to amorphous state systems, local school systems, schools themselves, and teachers as a collective mass. These systems and amorphous individuals receive generic blame for poor academic performance, but there is really no meaningful way to hold such a vastly segmented collection—there are some 17,000 plus school boards and 3.8 million teachers in the United States—of entities and individuals authentically responsible.

As the primary result, academic achievement has stagnated or only increased marginally and public education reform is catastrophically politicized.

Accredited postsecondary education institutions engender systemic dysfunction at the primary and secondary school levels by the admission of students who are not capable of gainful education and using funds appropriated for postsecondary education for remediation. This policy and practice vitiate accountability for educational achievement at the primary and secondary school level.

Admitting someone incapable of gainful education to an accredited postsecondary education institution is like awarding a gold star in an etiquette course to someone who still picks food out of his or her teeth with a fork.

The only valid way to exact accountability for literacy and numeracy at the primary and secondary school level is to deny admission to postsecondary institutions to anyone who does not evidence the intellectual capability and knowledge base for gainful education. Any eighteen year old who is literate and numerate upon completion of high school typically possesses the intellectual wherewithal to make an informed decision about a career path.

Many young people enter postsecondary education institutions lacking critical thinking and reasoning capability to confidently make a choice fitting their personalities and interests, and because they don't know what else to do. Too many drop out with student loan debt they cannot service and their future in a less secure state because they remain employable only at the margins.

Lack of literacy and numeracy self-evidently disqualifies anyone from making an informed decision about assuming an educational loan that can amount to tens of thousands of dollars.

Prison System Reform

Sentenced to Literacy and Numeracy

Any American who remains illiterate for a lifetime rarely possesses the capability to optimize his or her productivity for either personal benefit or for the benefit of society. One toxic consequence of illiteracy in the United States is a daily jail population of 2.4 million with another 10 million or so on parole or probation. Increases in correctional budgets increase the political power of the correctional industry, including its unions. We now spend nearly as much on corrections as we do on postsecondary education, and without substantive change, will continue to do so in the future.

The convicted are largely illiterate when they committed the crime(s), are illiterate while incarcerated, and are illiterate upon release.

Just as every student admitted to the postsecondary education system must be able to realize gainful education without remediation, no prisoner of the criminal justice system—those serving sentences longer than one year who otherwise qualify for release on the condition of time served—should be released unless they pass a baseline literacy test. Every sentence beyond one year must include the requirement that the individual manifest literacy, and to improve behavior, must include those with life and death penalty sentences.

Sentences will lengthen automatically for those sentenced until they satisfy this requirement. (The clinically mentally ill, incapable of learning, and with organic brain damage may be exempted.) Those on parole and probation must the literacy requirement as a condition of satisfying their respective sentences.

Courses necessary to establish literacy and numeracy must be provided online to minimize capital costs and maximize success while not compromising or threatening the security of any individual or institution. Lack of intellectual self-esteem and ability to reason due to illiteracy is the principal cause of crippling recidivism rates in federal, state, and local correctional systems.

Guaranteeing Capability for Gainful Education

Primary and secondary educational reform in the United States is hideously politicized. Reformers are legion: presidents, governors, and politicians of all stripes, school boards, parents, and concerned citizens. American twentieth and twenty-first century history evidences, quite startlingly however, that political, ideological, and sectarian reform of public education is a circular firing squad.

Virtually all reforms arising from political action will be jettisoned when political power—the outcome of the latest fashionable effort—inevitably shifts. Even valuable reforms are doomed when administrators and teachers receive marching orders from the newest educational power-that-be; they know that funds for the previous reform have vanished.

One way to effect durable and lasting educational reform is to establish a national computer-mediated learning system parallel to the existing K-12 public education system to help ensure that every student evidences the capability for gainful education upon graduation from high school.

The parallel system is not a replacement for the existing public system; students participate in the computer-mediated system outside regular school hours. In the parallel system, each student is the measure of success or failure; there is no aggregation of test scores.

Academic content must be an amalgam of the best generic content across the curriculum. Courses will be available nationally without regard to economic status, integrity of family unit, or geographic location. All students must be tested to ascertain what they know and don't know prior to enrollment in each discrete course, and tested again upon completion of the course.

Those failing to manifest acceptable improvement will be allowed to take the course again at no cost. No letter or numerical grade will be given, and no certificates, diplomas, or degrees will be awarded. Academic achievements of the students will redound to the K-12 schools in which they are enrolled through improved academic performance.

Parents won't have to ask what their kid learned at school because they will already know.

Informed knowledge of student academic performance verified through objective testing—once a critical mass is reached in each school—is the foundation for substantive reform. As long as parental, guardian, and public concern over K-12 performance remains atomized because the absence of a uniform knowledge about individual student performance, no long lasting change can be effected.

The Tipping Point

If we fail to take steadfast action immediately to materially reform our entire education system in the United States, our nation will continue to be besieged with illiteracy, massive expenditures on corrections, college graduates with unaffordable education debt, and working adults without college degrees.

Our education system is at the tipping point. If we allow it to go over, it will prove virtually impossible to right it.

APPENDIX

The Butterball Effect

Butterball was a young, warm-hearted, irresistibly concupiscent, full-bodied prostitute in a rural French city whose leaders received ominous warning the Prussian army was about to invade.

Early one morning, jammed cheek to cheek and jowl to jowl in a coach drawn by a team of powerful horses, were eight of the town's most upright and reputable citizens: an exceedingly successful wine merchant and wife; a very wealthy businessman and wife; a powerful political leader and wife, and two pock-marked, dumpy nuns. They received each other genially and were eager to be away from approaching harm. Doors were long closed, but the coach hadn't moved a wheel length.

All repeatedly shared anxious looks; this was no time to dally.

Suddenly, a door was yanked open.

Physical queasiness, hot embarrassment, and stone-cold silence greeted cheery Butterball as she clambered up into the coach, manhandling a gargantuan wicker basket and suffusing the interior with the scent of cheap toilet water.

Three husbands received withering looks from their wives that brought no respite from the utterly scandalous presence of Butterball. The men—each knew Butterball personally other than by reputation—kept their eyes averted from their wives, the nuns, and Butterball.

Stomachs growling after seemingly endless emotionally jarring, physically crowded, tight-lipped hours in the noisy, dusty, bumpy coach, each of the three couples—none of whom ever missed a meal in their lives—independently realized that, in the rush to escape, they neglected to bring anything to eat or drink.

It was too dangerous to stop, and they were consumed with the sheer horror of involuntary fasting until they arrived at their intended destination later that evening.

Suddenly, as if on an African savannah, nostrils flared, eyes narrowed, and eight heads snapped toward the satanic, alien, wicker basket open on Butterball's ample lap.

The couples and the nuns peered inside with unconcealed lust.

There—as if pumping lifeblood like an Olympian heart—was a lavish array of the most appetizing food they had in their lives ever seen: roasted chickens; legs of lamb; a giant ham; plump sausages; pungent cheese; freshly baked bread; scrumptious-looking desserts, and, dear Lord . . . wine.

Butterball, smacking her voluptuous lips after sucking a chunk of meat off a plump chicken drumstick, suddenly noticed the haunted, desperate looks on her exceedingly well fed, but presently starving companions.

Without hesitation, she offered to share the contents of her basket with her fellow refugees. Instantly, her nose-in-the-air, gargoyle-like fellow travelers transmogrified into smiling, giddy, and, it cannot go without saying, eternally grateful and convivial diners certain to remain devoted friends.

Soon, everyone's lips smacked to the same beat.

Immediately following the inhalation of the providential feast came luxurious, narcotic-like slumber for the husbands. Stomachs stretched beatifically, even the wives restrained themselves from sharply elbowing their obnoxiously snoring mates. Butterball, rosy cheeks filled with good cheer and warmth, grinned happily.

Barely discernable smiles even broke the histrionic abstemiousness that normally kept the expressions of the two nuns in tight check.

Gratitude and warmth toward Butterball had cooled noticeably by the time the coach reached the inn where the refugees from the Prussian army would spend the night. Studiously ignored at dinner, Butterball watched wide-eyed as her coach companions—in miraculous, cacophonous union—abruptly all pushed themselves up from the dining table by the arms of their heavy wooden chairs.

Suddenly, the room filled with an advance company of Prussian dragoons led by a dashing young lieutenant whose eyes instantly lit up at the sight of Butterball.

Her reputation had preceded her.

A dark cloud passed over Butterball's happy countenance.

The lieutenant brusquely ordered Butterball to follow him. Butterball's jaw set, and her body hardened. When he turned back at the door to see if she obeyed his order, she glowered fiercely at him.

Four dragoons had to struggle mightily to carry her through the door into the hallway.

Butterball's fellow patriots shared at first resentful, then increasingly anxious looks as they eavesdropped on the heated argument between Butterball and the lieutenant—astounded they were that she spoke fluent German—outside the hallway door, the four dragoons too spent to carry her further.

The eight former atheists in the foxhole quaked like cold, damp sheep when the stone-faced lieutenant suddenly appeared in the doorway.

"Butterball sleeps with me, you go free."

The three couples and the nuns instantly agreed that it would not prove wholesome to be there when the Prussian army arrived. The wine merchant announced convincingly that he would apply his considerable skills of persuasion to convince Butterball to accommodate the forgivable and, given their desperate circumstances, a really quite reasonable demand from someone everyone agrees is a very handsome young man who certainly has his human priorities in order.

The offer and explanation elevated the wine merchant's wife's bushy eyebrows to a supernatural height.

The peck-sniff wife of the political leader, in a dry, sandpapery voice, croaked that her devoted friend Butterball would not abandon them after being accorded the uncommon privilege of an intimate coach ride.

Less than five minutes later, expression downcast, the wine merchant sloughed disconsolately back into the room.

"Butterball's a patriot and will have nothing to do with him."

The wives, without the slightest hint to each other, independently tore pell-mell toward the hall door and squeezed through simultaneously in an unseemly squall of rustling garments, shrieks, and squawks.

Huddled in the hallway outside Butterball's room shushing each other, they agreed to pledge her their lifelong adoration.

"God placed the power of life and death in her loins," the horse-faced wife of the wealthy businessman whinnied before she blew her long nose.

Creating a deep rut on the edge of her bed, Butterball swooned with the touching flattery of her three new—oddly unpatriotic—wealthy friends. Flattery and promises were to no avail.

Butterball was adamant: "Vive la France!"

At an almost imperceptible nod from the chinless wife of the wine merchant, all smiling woodenly, the wives backed out of the room without having to determine the location of the door.

The dusky nuns listening to the entreaties of the terrified couples were reminded of the generous financial contributions made to the church, and were alerted—most felicitously—as to the primitive sexual prejudices of young, uneducated, dragooned peasant Prussian soldiers.

Eyes clearer than they had ever in their lives been, the nuns forsook their hard-core belief that the sins of the flesh deserved the eternal fires of hell and whisked off to convince Butterball it was her God-given duty to commit what, in any other circumstance but the instant one, was a mortal sin.

The infinite and mysterious ways of the Lord are not always comprehensible by mere human beings; witness the God-given power of a prodigious sinner over the lives of eight simple, innocent, credulous, God-fearing Christians.

The next morning, the couples and the nuns were nestled safely in the coach with the doors shut when one was suddenly yanked open.

Butterball raised a foot to climb up and the inhabitants withered.

Quickly gathering his wits, the wine merchant signaled for Butterball to step back as if he might assist her, slammed the door, locked it, and banged sharply on the roof.

The driver cracked his whip and the coach rumbled off in a fury of hoof beats.

Butterball was alone with her empty wicker basket.

APPENDIX

North Central Commission on Institutions of Higher Education Paper on Regional Accreditation Issues Distributed by the Staff of the Arizona Board of Regents

Arizona regents' rationale for transfer of accreditation from North Central to the Western Association of Schools and Colleges lamented that regional accrediting associations were unequal in numbers of institutions affiliated, number of states in each region, and geographic areas encompassed.

These disparities allegedly caused the North Central Association to abandon its standards.

Dr. Thurston Manning, executive director of the Commission on Institutions of Higher Education authored North Central's response to the rationale offered by the Arizona regents' in support of the accreditation region transfer.

> *The six regional associations are indeed unequal in numbers . . . This is the result of complex historical forces that need not be described here. The end result*

> *is not unlike the pattern of state boundaries, and both patterns can be criticized on the same grounds: Texas is too large, Rhode Island is too small; California is too populous and Nevada too sparsely settled; New York too wealthy and Alabama too poor. But no one would seriously propose redrawing state boundaries: whatever forces determined the boundaries in the past are immaterial to the traditions and customs that have developed within each state since its formation.*[111]

The regent's staff paper asserted North Central abandoned educational standards compared to those of the Western, Northwestern, and Southern Associations, which possessed explicit accreditation standards and honorably applied them.

> *The discussion . . . suggesting substantial differences between (the standards) of regional associations . . . is a gross distortion. [In 1930] (I)ncreasing concerns of the rigidity [of explicit standards] . . . imposed on colleges, together with the experience derived from granting exceptions, led to an extended study of these standards and their relation to educational quality, The NCA [North Central Association] Study [published in the NCA Quarterly and University of Chicago Press], remains the most elaborate and careful study of this relationship. Its conclusion is that standards are not well associated with educational quality, and cannot be used satisfactorily to judge educational quality. The 1934 study led the NCA to adopt the principle that each institution should be judged on its success in achieving its own well defined, publicly stated, and educationally appropriate purposes. The soundness of the NCA study resulted in the adoption of this*

> *principle by all other regional commissions dealing with colleges and universities. Every postsecondary regional commission today continues to subscribe to this principle. The WASC constitution (article IV, Section 1), requires each WASC commission to adopt criteria for certification which "shall provide for the evaluation of each institution on the basis to the degree to which it is accomplishing the purposes and functions outlined in its own statement of objectives . . . and on the appropriateness of those purposes and functions.*[112]

All six regional accrediting associations adopted this core evaluation principle, and publicly so attested in their accreditation guidelines. North Central observed the principal absolutely; WASC observed it as long as the institution was conformed traditionally.

> *A requirement of recognition of the Council on Postsecondary Accreditation [COPA] is that the accrediting commission judges each institution against its own purposes. The COPA "Provisions and Procedures for becoming recognized as an Accrediting Agency" requires that a COPA-recognized agency "recognize the right of institutions or programs to be evaluated in light of their own stated purposes."*[113]

The regents, and WASC, through confirmation of its support for the transfer of Arizona's accreditation to the WASC region, claimed that North Central's failure to employ the word *standards* meant that it had no standards.

Manning noted that although other regionals, including WASC, employ the word *standards* in the description of their accreditation criteria, the word used in the context of accreditation that proceeds from the evaluation construct that each institution be judged in light of the purposes it has established for itself is, in the universe of institutional accreditation, a misnomer.

> *(C)onsider the faculty, library, and student services "standards" of the WASC Senior Commission: Members of the faculty are qualified by training and experience to serve at the levels that the institution's purposes require. The library holdings and other learning resources are sufficient in quantity, depth, diversity, and currentness to support all of the institution's academic offerings at appropriate levels. Student services are available to support the objectives of the educational programs. It is obvious that in each of these essential components of an institution the institution is to be judged against its own purposes. In no case has there been set external standards that each institution must comply with. These are not "objective standards,"[as the Regent's staff paper alleges] . . . and so describing WASC procedures does an injustice to them by implying that WASC follows an outdated and unacceptable accreditation process."*[114]

WASC—evidenced by the procedure it had established for the fraudulent accreditation of the programs of accredited out-of-state colleges and schools operating in California and use of "objective evaluation standards"—violated not only the scope of its accrediting authority by accrediting the "programs" or "operations" of six out-of-state institutions, but the very criteria it professed to observe in its recognition as a regional accrediting association.

WASC would unlikely judge University of Phoenix by the degree to which it achieved the educationally appropriate goals it established for itself because WASC then rarely differentiated between the traditional eighteen-to-twenty-four-year-old full-time student and the working adult student who worked full time. WASC commonly judged institutions against highly prescriptive standards appropriate to a traditional higher education institution serving younger, full-time students on a single campus.

> *To summarize: all of the regional accrediting commissions judge an institution and its component parts against the stated purposes of the institution. The utilization of "standards" by some commissions is simply a particular way of providing guidance to institutions and evaluation teams to help ensure comprehensive evaluations.*[115]

APPENDIX

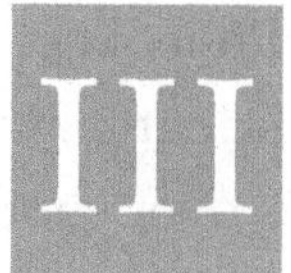

2000—2013 Regulatory, Legislative, and Legal Actions with the University of Phoenix and Apollo Group

YEAR

1999 The University of Phoenix fined $650,000[116] by the U.S. Department of Education for allegedly violating student reimbursement regulations.

2000 University of Phoenix fined $6 million[117] by the U.S. Department of Education for alleged violation of instructional hours.

2003 A whistleblower lawsuit claim for illegally compensating recruiters based solely on the number of enrollments.

2004 A false claim lawsuit alleged payment of illegal financial incentives to student recruiters, wrongful pressure on recruiters to enroll students, and concealment of illegal practices. University of Phoenix was fined $9.8[118] million by U.S. Department of Education, and $3.5[119] million by the U.S. Department of Labor.

2007 University of Phoenix eligibility for federally guaranteed student loans placed on month-to-month basis over continuing the U.S. Department of Education concern about student-enrollment practices.

2008 Apollo Group was required to post a $125 million letter of credit[120] with the U.S. Department of Education arising from continuing concerns about enrollment practices that admitted students with little or no knowledge of their educational responsibilities or understanding of the meaning and responsibilities of student financial aid.

2009 2003 Whistleblower lawsuit settled for $67 million plus $11 million in legal fees.[121]

2011 U.S. Supreme Court rejected Apollo Group's appeal of a $277.5 million class action award upheld by the Ninth Circuit Court of Appeals.

2011 Apollo Group settles 2003 whistleblower lawsuit—original award $277.5 million—for $145 million.[122]

2013 North Central Higher Learning Commission evaluation team recommends University of Phoenix accreditation be placed on probation.

Endnotes

1 Machiavelli, Nicolo, *The Prince,* Bantam Books, 1966.

2 Miller, James E., *Henry James, Theory of Fiction,* University of Nebraska Press, 1971.

3 Fadiman, Clifton, *Collected Writings of Ambrose Bierce,* Citadel Press, N.Y., 1974, p. 192.

4 Apollo Group, *Apollo Group Prospectus,* Smith Barney Inc., Alex. Brown & Sons, December 5, 1994, p. 3.

5 *For Profit Higher Education: The Failure to Safeguard the Federal Investment and Ensure Student Success,* United States Senate Health, Education, Labor, and Pensions Committee (HELP) Report, p. 85.

6 *For Profit Higher Education,* Senate HELP Report, p. 26.

7 Apollo Group, *Prospectus,* Smith Barney Inc., Alex. Brown & Sons, December 5, 1994, p. 30.

8 University of Phoenix Consumer Information Guide, 2011—2012, Summary of Undergraduate Graduation Rates After Six Years.

9 U.S. Department of Education, Institute of Education Sciences, National Center for Educational Statistics, Online Search, April 22, 2013.

10 2007 and 2008, University of Phoenix Annual Academic Report; 2009, U.S. Department of Education.

11 *For Profit Higher Education,* Senate HELP Report, p. 29.

12 See Appendix III, p. 238.

13 Mark Brenner, Senior Vice President for External Affairs, Apollo Group, Email, March 29, 2013.

14 Susan E. Van Kollenburg, Higher Learning Commission, North Central Association of Colleges and Schools, Email, March 6, 2013.

15 *For Profit Higher Education,* Senate HELP Report, Appendices, pp. A-20-1, A21-1, A22-1.

16 *Chronicle of Higher Education,* February 11, 2011.

17 *Chronicle of Higher Education,* February 11, 2011.

18 *Chronicle of Higher Education,* February 11, 2011.

19 Insider Trading Activities at Apollo Group, http://www.insider-monitor.com/trading/cik928887.html

20 University of Phoenix Annual Academic Report, 2011.

21 *'Quick-degrees' college in line for accreditation, Arizona Republic,* November 27, 1977.

22 Editorial, Television Station KNTV, San Jose, California, September 1973.

23 John G. Sperling, *Rebel With a Cause,* John Wiley & Sons, 1997, p. 56.

24 *Rebel With a Cause,* pp. 69, 70.

25 *Rebel With a Cause,* p. 78.

26 *Rebel With a Cause.* p. 79.

27 *Rebel With a Cause,* p. 123.

28 *Rebel With a Cause,* p. 105

29 Maupassant, Guy de, *A Parisian Affair and Other Stories,* Penguin Books, London, 2004, pp. 1-40.

30 *Rebel With a Cause,* p. 96

31 *Rebel With a Cause,* p. 109.

32 *Rebel With a Cause,* p. 104.

33 University of Phoenix, *Self-Study Report Submitted to the North Central Association of Colleges and Schools*, December 1977, revised, March 1978, pp. 19, 20.

34 Self-Study Report, p. 20.

35 Carnegie Commission on Higher Education, *New Students and New Places: Policies for Future Growth and Development of Higher Education*, 1971, p. 39.

36 University of Phoenix, *Self-Study Report Submitted to the North Central Association of Colleges and Schools, 1977*, pp. 27, 28.

37 Self Study Report, p. 28.

38 Self-Study Report, p. 55.

39 Self-Study Report, p. 55.

40 *Arizona Republic*, May 11, 1977.

41 Arizona Board of Regents transcript, November 25, 1977.

42 Arizona Board of Regents transcript, November 26, 1977.

43 Arizona Board of Regents transcript, November 26, 1977.

44 Lois Broyles, *Phoenix Gazette*, November 26, 1977.

45 Uvey Miner, ASU *State Press*, November 29, 1977.

46 Uvey Miner, ASU *State Press*, November 29, 1977.

47 Mary Connell, ASU *State Press*, December 1, 1977.

48 Cecilia Goodnow, *Arizona Republic*, January 3, 1978.

49 *Phoenix Gazette*, January 11, 1978.

50 Attributed to Mark Twain.

51 *Arizona Republic*, March 17, 1978.

52 *Rebel With a Cause*, pp. 112, 113.

53 Self-Study Report, p. 107.

54 *Rebel With a Cause*, p. 110.

55 *Rebel With a Cause*, p. 113.

56 *Rebel With a Cause*, p. 114.

57 *Rebel With a Cause,* p. 115.

58 *Rebel With a Cause,* p. 117.

59 *Rebel With a Cause,* p. 118.

60 *Rebel With a Cause,* p. 119.

61 Report of Jane McVey, Office of the Republican Majority Leader.

62 *Report on Transfer of Credit to State Universities,* House Staff Report, pp. 18, 35.

63 Arizona House Bill (HB) 2115, p. 2.

64 *Rebel With a Cause,* pp. 121—122.

65 *Rebel With a Cause,* p. 137.

66 *Rebel With a Cause,* pp. 137—139.

67 *Rebel With a Cause,* p. 139.

68 The *Arizona Republic,* December 17, 1978.

69 *Rebel With a Cause,* p. 144.

70 *Rebel With a Cause,* p. 145.

71 *Rebel With a Cause,* p. 146.

72 Order, Civil Action No. 181-JM-2177, 1984, United States District Court for the District of Colorado, August 13, 1984, pp. 6, 7.

73 Order, Civil Action No. 81-JM-2177, p. 4.

74 Order, Civil Action No. 81-JM-2177, p. 5.

75 Order, Civil Action No, 81-JM-2177, p. 7.

76 *UOP v Sacramento Union,* deposition of Dan Walters.

77 Dan Walters, "It's an Education in Politics," *Sacramento Union,* April 23, 1983.

78 "It's an Education in Politics."

79 "It's an Education in Politics."

80 "It's an Education in Politics."

81 Steven A. Capps, "Campaign to Block 'Diploma Mill' Law

has Strong Backer," *San Francisco Examiner*, May 1, 1983.

82 Michael Scott-Blair, "Accreditation is tense, emotional issue," *San Diego Union*, June 24, 1984.

83 Opinion, California Attorney General. 1984.

84 *Los Angeles Times*, February 29, 1980, June 4, 1980, and September 23, 1980.

85 *Los Angeles Times*, July 17, 1980.

86 National Association of Trade and Technical Schools.

87 Association of Independent Colleges and Schools.

88 National Home Study Council.

89 New England, North Central, Middle States, Southern, Northwest.

90 Licensed by California Office of Private Postsecondary Education.

91 *Rebel With a Cause*, p. 150.

92 *Rebel With a Cause*, p. 176.

93 *Rebel With a Cause*, p. 175.

94 *Rebel With a Cause*, p. 175.

95 *Rebel With a Cause*, p. 148.

96 *Rebel With a Cause*, p. 177.

97 *Rebel With a Cause*, p. 175.

98 *Rebel With a Cause*, p.176.

99 "Education Department Orders U. of Phoenix to Pay $650,000," *Chronicle of Higher Education*, August 13, 1999.

100 Regulatory, Legislative, and Legal Fines, Judgments, and Actions Against University of Phoenix and Apollo Groups, See Appendix III, p. 257.

101 *For Profit Higher Education*, Senate HELP Report, p. 1.

102 *For Profit Higher Education*, Senate HELP Report, p. 86.

103 *Wall Street Journal*, March 5, 2013.

104 *For Profit Higher Education,* Senate HELP Report, p. 1.

105 *For Profit Higher Education,* Senate HELP Report, p. 2.

106 *For Profit Higher Education,* Senate HELP Report, p. 7.

107 "Higher Education—Not What It Used To Be," *The Economist,* December 1, 2012, p. 29.

108 *Wall Street Journal,* November 23, 2012.

109 "The Cost of College: It's Off the Charts," *Bloomberg Businessweek,* August 27—September 2, 2012, p. 20.

110 *U.S. Education Reform and National Security,* Independent Task Force No. 38, Council on Foreign Affairs, 2012.

111 Dr. Thurston Manning, Response to the Arizona Board of Regents, Staff Paper, 1981, p. 1.

112 Manning, p. 2.

113 Manning, p. 2.

114 Manning, p. 3.

115 Manning, p. 4.

116 "Education Department Orders U. of Phoenix to Pay $650,000, *Chronicle of Higher Education,* August 13, 1999.

117 "University Owner Settles Federal Suit Over Student Aid," *New York Times,* May 14, 2000.

118 "Student Recruitment Tactics at the University of Phoenix Blasted by Feds University of Phoenix Audit Leads to $9.8 mil Fine," *Arizona Republic,* September 14, 2004.

119 "University of Phoenix, Department of Labor Reach Overtime Agreement," *Phoenix Business Journal,* July 23, 2004.

120 "Apollo Repaid Education Aid Late, Gave Lax Counseling," *Businessweek,* January 10, 2010

121 "Apollo Group Settles Suit for $78.5 Million," *Arizona Republic,* December 15, 2009.

122 *In Re Apollo Group, Inc. Securities Litigation,* No. 04-2147. D. Ariz.

Made in the USA
Las Vegas, NV
13 January 2021

15857446R00157